An Analysis of

Geoffrey Parker's

Global Crisis
War, Climate Change and Catastrophe in the Seventeenth Century

Ian Jackson

www.macat.com
info@macat.com

Cover illustration: Etienne Gilfillan

Cataloguing in Publication Data
A catalogue record for this book is available from the British Library.
Library of Congress Cataloguing-in-Publication Data is available upon request.

ISBN 978-1-912302-73-4 (hardback)
ISBN 978-1-912128-08-2 (paperback)
ISBN 978-1-912281-61-9 (e-book)

Notice
The information in this book is designed to orientate readers of the work under analysis,
to elucidate and contextualise its key ideas and themes, and to aid in the development
of critical thinking skills. It is not meant to be used, nor should it be used, as a
substitute for original thinking or in place of original writing or research. References and
notes are provided for informational purposes and their presence does not constitute
endorsement of the information or opinions therein. This book is presented solely for
educational purposes. It is sold on the understanding that the publisher is not engaged
to provide any scholarly advice. The publisher has made every effort to ensure that
this book is accurate and up-to-date, but makes no warranties or representations with
regard to the completeness or reliability of the information it contains. The information
and the opinions provided herein are not guaranteed or warranted to produce particular
results and may not be suitable for students of every ability. The publisher shall not be
liable for any loss, damage or disruption arising from any errors or omissions, or from
the use of this book, including, but not limited to, special, incidental, consequential or
other damages caused, or alleged to have been caused, directly or indirectly, by the
information contained within.

CONTENTS

WAYS IN TO THE TEXT

Who Is Geoffrey Parker?   9

What Does *Global Crisis* Say?   10

Why Does *Global Crisis* Matter?   12

SECTION 1: INFLUENCES

Module 1: The Author and the Historical Context   15

Module 2: Academic Context   20

Module 3: The Problem   25

Module 4: The Author's Contribution   30

SECTION 2: IDEAS

Module 5: Main Ideas   35

Module 6: Secondary Ideas   41

Module 7: Achievement   46

Module 8: Place in the Author's Work   51

SECTION 3: IMPACT

Module 9: The First Responses   57

Module 10: The Evolving Debate   62

Module 11: Impact and Influence Today   67

Module 12: Where Next?   72

Glossary of Terms   77

People Mentioned in the Text   85

Works Cited   92

THE MACAT LIBRARY

The Macat Library is a series of unique academic explorations of seminal works in the humanities and social sciences – books and papers that have had a significant and widely recognised impact on their disciplines. It has been created to serve as much more than just a summary of what lies between the covers of a great book. It illuminates and explores the influences on, ideas of, and impact of that book. Our goal is to offer a learning resource that encourages critical thinking and fosters a better, deeper understanding of important ideas.

Each publication is divided into three Sections: Influences, Ideas, and Impact. Each Section has four Modules. These explore every important facet of the work, and the responses to it.

This Section-Module structure makes a Macat Library book easy to use, but it has another important feature. Because each Macat book is written to the same format, it is possible (and encouraged!) to cross-reference multiple Macat books along the same lines of inquiry or research. This allows the reader to open up interesting interdisciplinary pathways.

To further aid your reading, lists of glossary terms and people mentioned are included at the end of this book (these are indicated by an asterisk [*] throughout) – as well as a list of works cited.

Macat has worked with the University of Cambridge to identify the elements of critical thinking and understand the ways in which six different skills combine to enable effective thinking.
Three allow us to fully understand a problem; three more give us the tools to solve it. Together, these six skills make up the **PACIER** model of critical thinking. They are:

ANALYSIS – understanding how an argument is built
EVALUATION – exploring the strengths and weaknesses of an argument
INTERPRETATION – understanding issues of meaning

CREATIVE THINKING – coming up with new ideas and fresh connections
PROBLEM-SOLVING – producing strong solutions
REASONING – creating strong arguments

To find out more, visit **WWW.MACAT.COM.**

CRITICAL THINKING AND *GLOBAL CRISIS*

Primary critical thinking skill: ANALYSIS
Secondary critical thinking skill: REASONING

Few historians can claim to have undertaken historical analysis on as grand a scale as Geoffrey Parker did in his 2013 work *Global Crisis: War, Climate Change and Catastrophe in the Seventeenth Century*: a doorstop of a book that surveys the 'general crisis of the 17th century,' shows that it was experienced practically throughout the world, and was not merely a European phenomenon, and links it to the impact of climate change in the form of the advent of a cold period known as the 'Little Ice Age.'

Parker's triumph is made possible by the deployment of formidable critical thinking skills – reasoning, to construct an engaging overall argument from very disparate material, and analysis, to re-examine and understand the plethora of complex secondary sources on which his book is built. In critical thinking, analysis is all about understanding the features and structures of argument: how given reasons lead to conclusions, and what kinds of implicit reasons and assumptions are being used. Historical analysis applies the same skills to the fabric of history, asking how given chains of events occur, how different reasons and factors interact, and so on.

Parker, though, takes things further than most in his quest to understand the meaning of a century's-worth of turbulence spread across the whole globe. Beginning by breaking down the evidence for significant climatic cooling in the 17th-century (due to decreased solar activity), he moves on to detailed study of the effects the cooling had on societies and regimes across the world. From this detailed spadework, he constructs a persuasive argument that accounts for the different ways in which the effects of climate change played out across the century – an argument with profound implications for a future likely to see serious climate change of its own.

ABOUT THE AUTHOR OF THE ORIGINAL WORK

Geoffrey Parker was born in 1943 in Nottingham, and read history at Christ's College, University of Cambridge. He went on to hold a series of posts at universities in Europe, Canada, and the United States. Before tackling climate change, Parker was a distinguished scholar of early modern history with particular interests in Spain and the history of warfare. He moved to Ohio State University in 1997, where he is the Andreas Dorpalen Professor of European History. *Global Crisis* is a key text for anyone involved in the worldwide debate on the impact of climate change.

ABOUT THE AUTHOR OF THE ANALYSIS

Ian Jackson is a PhD student in the Politics, Philosophy and Religion department at Lancaster University. He is interested in the role new media plays in the dissemination of ideas.

ABOUT MACAT

GREAT WORKS FOR CRITICAL THINKING

Macat is focused on making the ideas of the world's great thinkers accessible and comprehensible to everybody, everywhere, in ways that promote the development of enhanced critical thinking skills.

It works with leading academics from the world's top universities to produce new analyses that focus on the ideas and the impact of the most influential works ever written across a wide variety of academic disciplines. Each of the works that sit at the heart of its growing library is an enduring example of great thinking. But by setting them in context – and looking at the influences that shaped their authors, as well as the responses they provoked – Macat encourages readers to look at these classics and game-changers with fresh eyes. Readers learn to think, engage and challenge their ideas, rather than simply accepting them.

"Macat offers an amazing first-of-its-kind tool for interdisciplinary learning and research. Its focus on works that transformed their disciplines and its rigorous approach, drawing on the world's leading experts and educational institutions, opens up a world-class education to anyone."

Andreas Schleicher
Director for Education and Skills, Organisation for Economic Co-operation and Development

'Macat is taking on some of the major challenges in university education … They have drawn together a strong team of active academics who are producing teaching materials that are novel in the breadth of their approach.'

Prof Lord Broers,
former Vice-Chancellor of the University of Cambridge

'The Macat vision is exceptionally exciting. It focuses upon new modes of learning which analyse and explain seminal texts which have profoundly influenced world thinking and so social and economic development. It promotes the kind of critical thinking which is essential for any society and economy. This is the learning of the future.'

Rt Hon Charles Clarke, former UK Secretary of State for Education

'The Macat analyses provide immediate access to the critical conversation surrounding the books that have shaped their respective discipline, which will make them an invaluable resource to all of those, students and teachers, working in the field.'

Professor William Tronzo, University of California at San Diego

WAYS IN TO THE TEXT

KEY POINTS

- Richard J. Herrnstein (1930–1994) was an American experimental psychologist;* Charles Murray (b. 1943) is an American conservative* political scientist* (a scholar of political behavior and systems of government, holding right-wing political beliefs).

- *The Bell Curve* argues that inequality in America is the result of varying levels of intelligence in the population. The authors say that intelligence is the best predictor of success in life.

- *The Bell Curve* is one of the most controversial books of the twentieth century. It claims that there are large differences in intelligence between ethnic groups* (subgroups who self-identify as Latino, black, white, or Asian, for example).

Who are Richard J. Herrnstein and Charles Murray?

The son of Hungarian Jewish immigrants, Richard J. Herrnstein, coauthor of *The Bell Curve: Intelligence and Class Structure in American Life* (1994), was born in 1930. He grew up in New York City, going on to Harvard University* to study for a PhD in experimental psychology.* At Harvard he worked with the famous psychologist B. F. Skinner.*[1] Skinner was a founder of the school of behaviorism, according to which all human behaviors are conditioned by rewards and punishments.[2] Later, however, after completing his PhD and joining the Harvard faculty as an experimental psychologist, Herrnstein moved away from Skinner's ideas. He became a leading researcher on intelligence and human behavior and claimed that innate (that is, inherent or inborn) biological forces contribute more to human behavior than one's environment.

Charles Murray was born in Newton, Iowa in 1943. He attended Harvard as an undergraduate and earned his PhD in political science at Massachusetts Institute of Technology.* During the 1980s he was a fellow at the Manhattan Institute for Policy Research,* a conservative think tank* (a privately funded organization conducting research and advocating for policy change). Here he wrote *Losing Ground: American Social Policy, 1950–1980* (1984), a book that made him famous in conservative intellectual circles. In 1990, Murray joined the American Enterprise Institute,* another conservative think tank in Washington, DC.

Four years later, Murray and Herrnstein collaborated on *The Bell Curve: Intelligence and Class Structure in American Life*. Shortly before the book was published, Herrnstein died of lung cancer. When *The Bell Curve* was met with both acclaim and controversy for its arguments and views, it was left to Murray to defend the book. He remains a staunch defender of the work's most controversial claims and has become one of America's most prominent conservative intellectuals.

What Does **The Bell Curve** Say?

The Bell Curve presents a controversial argument. The book's core idea is that social inequality in America can be explained by genes*— material inherited by children from their parents conferring biological characteristics. Herrnstein and Murray believe that intelligence is the most reliable predictor of success in life. At the top, the intellectual elite graduate from the best colleges and hold the best jobs. At the bottom, the intellectual underclass* suffers poverty, crime, and unemployment.

According to Herrnstein and Murray, intelligence is predominantly an inherited attribute. In the simplest terms, either you are born smart or you are not. Neither home environment nor schooling can change your genetic* inheritance.

The intellectual elite was fortunate enough to be born with good genes. The intellectual underclass was less fortunate in the genetic lottery. Between these two groups, *The Bell Curve* suggests, there is a growing gap, and there is little that the federal government can do about it. The authors believe that policies to improve opportunities for the lower classes will not achieve their goals because intelligence, not education or environment, determines people's success in life.

Herrnstein and Murray suggest that the intellectual divide in the population lies at the heart of the socioeconomic divide. An individual's socioeconomic status* is based on their economic status and their social position. This social gap (the divide between those who have wealth and influence and those who do not) also happens to mirror racial divides in America. Herrnstein and Murray link social position to genetic inheritance, which therefore links intelligence to race*—and offers an intellectual justification of the dominance of white people in American society.

When the book was first published these views about the social–racial divides in modern America were widely criticized. *The Bell Curve* became one of the most controversial publications of the 1990s.

Three decades on, *The Bell Curve* is still controversial. Policy-makers and researchers continue to ask questions raised by the book:

- Is the intellectual underclass incapable of the same success as the intellectual elite?*

- Is there a reason why African Americans are found in large numbers in impoverished communities?

- Is there nothing we can do to change this troubling reality?

By linking inequality, race, and intelligence, *The Bell Curve* provides a provocative explanation of how America's class structure formed in the twentieth century. It also provides a provocative explanation of why current social welfare* policies—policies designed to assist the poor by ensuring a measure of economic protection—are unlikely to change things.

The Bell Curve sold over 400,000 copies within months of its publication. Countless articles were published either denouncing or praising the book. A *New York Times* writer called the book "racial pornography."[3] Another writer praised Herrnstein and Murray for their courage in challenging political correctness.[4] *The Bell Curve* captured the attention of a divided nation. Few books since have placed such difficult and polarizing questions into the mainstream in such a way. While much of the clamor has passed, questions about inequality, genes, and social policy remain. *The Bell Curve* gives readers an insight into how these questions will continue to challenge our notions of equality, race, and social justice.

Why Does **The Bell Curve** Matter?

It would be difficult to overstate the impact made by *The Bell Curve*. Perhaps the most debated book of 1994, it can be read as a portrait of America at its most divided. Critics of the book raced to disprove the link between intelligence, genetics, and race. Supporters were just as quick to claim that Herrnstein and Murray had put their finger on the true source of social disparities. A large portion of recent psychology* and social science* research looks at responses to the book. For this reason, one historian described *The Bell Curve* as a "phenomenon … more than a mere book."[5] Given the intensity of the response on all sides, it is important to see what Herrnstein and Murray actually say by looking at the original text.

The Bell Curve blends psychology (the study of the human mind and behavior), sociology* (the study of the history and nature of human society), and political science* (inquiry into political behavior and governance). For those interested in history and policymaking, the book is an important document in "the culture wars"* between American liberals and American conservatives in the 1980s and 1990s—a series of high-profile debates on issues including affirmative action* (policies designed to ease inequality by increasing the employment prospects of disadvantaged citizens), welfare reform, and educational standards. Those interested in psychology will find provocative theses on the nature of intelligence. Is it actually measurable? Does it explain human behavior? Can it change over time? The conservatism of Herrnstein and Murray will engage students of politics. *The Bell Curve* raises important questions about the politics of research. It presents a forceful argument against the federal government's ability to equalize life chances. Do changes in people's environments, through welfare or remedial education* programs (programs for underperforming, and often low-income, students), make them better students, parents, and workers?

Although scholars have failed to achieve consensus on *The Bell Curve's* scientific merits, and politicians continue to be divided on its policy recommendations, the book remains a testament to controversies surrounding intelligence, race, and class in twentieth-century America. In many ways, the debates over the nature of intelligence and its influence on behavior are still widespread. *The Bell Curve* suggests that social policies like affirmative action, universal preschool, and social welfare are ineffectual ways of solving the inequalities in American society. These policies continue to be objects of political debate. Given that, it is not surprising that the ideas in *The Bell Curve* continue to influence and inform opinions.

In 2012 Charles Murray published another book. *Coming Apart: The State of White America 1960–2010*⁶ reintroduced many themes from *The Bell Curve*. The book triggered further debates about America's future. As inequalities persist, and in some cases deepen, the importance of these questions grows. Engaging with *The Bell Curve* gives readers a chance to work these issues out for themselves.

NOTES

1   B. F. Skinner, *Beyond Freedom and Dignity* (New York: Vintage Books, 1972).

2   James Watson, "Psychology as a Behaviorist Views It," *Psychological Review* 20 (1913): 158–77.

3   Bob Herbert, "In America; Throwing a Curve," *The New York Times*, October 26, 1994.

4   Daniel Seligman, "Trashing *The Bell Curve*," *The National Review*, 46, no. 23 (1994), 60–1.

5   Andrew Hartman, *A War for the Soul of America: A History of the Culture Wars* (Chicago: University of Chicago Press, 2015), 115.

6   Charles Murray, *Coming Apart: The State of White America 1960–2010* (New York: Random House, 2012).

SECTION 1
INFLUENCES

MODULE 1
THE AUTHOR AND THE HISTORICAL CONTEXT

KEY POINTS

- *The Bell Curve* remains one of the most hotly debated works of twentieth-century social science* (the academic study of human beings and social groups).

- Herrnstein and Murray's provocative thesis links intelligence with race* and social success. Their book continues to provide a controversial explanation for why racial divides persist in American society.

- Herrnstein and Murray published *The Bell Curve* at the height of America's "culture wars"* between political liberals* and political conservatives* during the 1980s and 1990s.

Why Read This Text?

Richard J. Herrnstein and Charles Murray's book *The Bell Curve: Intelligence and Class Structure in American Life* (1994) wades into some of the most troubled waters in contemporary America. The book argues that social inequality* between ethnic groups*—people of European, African, or indigenous American ancestry, for example— has a biological basis.

According to Herrnstein and Murray, widening inequality in America in income, educational attainment, and employment is largely explained by the differences in cognitive ability* (roughly, intelligence) between individuals. They argue that intelligence is decided by our genes.* As different ethnic groups have different genes, our intelligence is also affected by our ethnicity. This provocative argument raises debates about race, politics, economics, family, education, and equality.

> **❝** Our partnership has led to a more compelling intellectual adventure and a deeper friendship than we could have imagined. Authorship is alphabetical; the work was symbiotic. **❞**
>
> Richard J. Herrnstein and Charles Murray, *The Bell Curve: Intelligence and Class Structure in American Life*

The Bell Curve was published in 1994, at the height of the American "culture wars*" of the 1980s and 1990s. These were high-profile debates between liberals and conservatives that spanned a whole range of contentious issues, including affirmative action* and welfare.* In this environment *The Bell Curve* was bound to elicit strong reactions.

An excerpt from the book was published on October 31, 1994 in *The New Republic,** a magazine with liberal leanings. It was accompanied by comments. The respected American psychologist Richard Nisbett* praised Herrnstein and Murray for having "written a book that deals with extraordinarily important issues, many of which have been considered too explosive to discuss in the public arena yet need to be aired." Nonetheless, he disputed the idea that there was a scholarly consensus on their key claims.[1] Other commentators stated their "repulsion" by the idea that racial inequality has a biological basis.

The book sold over 400,000 copies. While its central thesis failed to gain mainstream support, explanations for the racial character of inequality in America continue to occupy scholars and politicians.

Authors' Lives

Richard J. Herrnstein was an experimental psychologist*—someone engaged in inquiry into the human mind and behavior—at Harvard University.* The son of Hungarian Jewish immigrants, he grew up in New York City, and studied psychology* at the City College of New York.* He obtained a PhD in experimental psychology* at Harvard,[2] where he studied with the famed psychologist B. F. Skinner.*[3] A behaviorist, Skinner argued that any and all human behavior is the direct result of conditioning—the rewards and consequences that result from the way we behave.[4] Over time, these external forces (the rewards and consequences) reinforce particular ways of behaving. Ironically, despite the fact that Herrnstein's academic training focused on the role of external forces in shaping behavior, in *The Bell Curve* he argues that innate biological forces (our genes) play a key role in the way we behave. Shortly before the publication of *The Bell Curve*, Herrnstein lost his life to lung cancer.

Charles Murray grew up in Newton, Iowa. As an undergraduate he studied history at Harvard, before obtaining his PhD in political science* at the Massachusetts Institute of Technology.* Murray went on to work for private research organizations, including the American Institutes for Research* and the right-wing think tank* the American Enterprise Institute.* His political stance is right wing and libertarian* (that is, he argues for individual freedom and is opposed to government intervention in society). Murray has clear ideas about the intractable nature of social hierarchies* (differences between individuals and groups in things such as income, educational achievement, and employment), and the futility of government programs designed to redress them. These ideas surface throughout *The Bell Curve*, especially in the concluding chapter of the book.

Authors' Backgrounds

Neither Herrnstein nor Murray came from an upper-class background. They acquired public influence and prestigious employment through America's elite institutions of higher education. Their success, one argument would have it, is down to the meritocratic* system, inside which advancement is based solely on achievement and ability—that is, merit. The notion of a meritocracy underpins the American belief that a combination of talent and resolve will be rewarded with recognition and success. Herrnstein developed this thesis in his early book *IQ in the Meritocracy* (1973), where he argued that the division of American society into a cognitive elite and a cognitive lower class reflects biological differences in intelligence.[5] As the American education system became more refined in the twentieth century, universities were able to select those with the most talent and place them in positions of power and prestige, regardless of their origins. This idea is restated in the first section of *The Bell Curve*, "The Emergence of a Cognitive Elite."*

The idea that merit alone leads to achievement came under heavy criticism from those active in civil rights and women's movements—political activity that began in the 1960s and 1970s and that is engaged with the struggle to achieve equal rights for minorities and women. In the 1980s and 1990s a new set of challenges arose. Many, among them those who argued for the benefits of multiculturalism,* asked how "merit" should be defined, and who should define it. A "multicultural" society is a society composed of different cultural traditions, commonly belonging to different ethnic groups; those valuing the possibilities of such a society argued that the type of success Herrnstein and Murray had attained was unattainable for those from minority groups,* as these groups lacked recognition and representation in universities.

These debates grew sharper as American living standards fell. The economic fortunes of the working class steadily declined in the 1970s and 1980s. In the 1980s and 1990s, African American communities were facing record levels of crime, homelessness, and youth unemployment, as well as a growing income gap with white Americans. But in a meritocracy this highly unequal class structure could be conceived as a matter of individual responsibility. Was this position defensible?

NOTES

1   Richard Nisbett, "Blue Genes," *The New Republic,* October 31, 1994 (http://www.newrepublic.com/article/120890/tnr-staffers-and-others-respond-claims-bell-curve, accessed October 15, 2015).

2   Richard Baum, "Richard J. Herrnstein: A Memoir," *Behavioral Analysis* 17 (1994): 201–6.

3   B. F. Skinner, *Beyond Freedom and Dignity* (New York: Vintage Books, 1972).

4   James Watson, "Psychology as a Behaviorist Views It," *Psychological Review* 20 (1913): 158–77.

5   Richard J. Herrnstein, *IQ in the Meritocracy* (Boston: Little, Brown, 1973).

MODULE 2
ACADEMIC CONTEXT

KEY POINTS

- *The Bell Curve* suggests that inherited intelligence has been overlooked as an explanation for the persistent inequalities in American society.

- By the 1990s inequality had become a growing concern for American social scientists.* They worried about the social disharmony that would follow from having a permanent underclass*—a section of society occupying the lowest position in the nation's social hierarchy for generations with little chances of advancement.

- This debate had ignored the issue of intelligence. There were fears that discussing the notion of intelligence would lead to explosive and incendiary theories about inherent differences between ethnic groups.*

The Work in its Context

Richard J. Herrnstein and Charles Murray's *The Bell Curve: Intelligence and Class Structure in American Life* addresses both academic and political concerns. This reflects the backgrounds of the two authors. Academically, *The Bell Curve* is an attempt to revive a tradition that dates back to the English naturalist Charles Darwin* and the theory of evolution* in its use of modern statistical analysis and testing mechanisms to determine the distribution of traits among a population. Herrnstein and Murray were testing the distribution of intelligence. Many researchers had avoided this topic because it carried overtones of scientific racism* (the use of scientific methods to argue that some racial groups are superior to others).

The idea that intelligence is a stable, inherited ability stems back to

> ❝ We are not indifferent to the ways in which this book, wrongly conceived, might do harm. We have worried about them from the day we set to work. But there can be no real progress in solving America's problems when they are as misperceived as they are today. ❞
>
> Richard J. Herrnstein and Charles Murray, *The Bell Curve: Intelligence and Class Structure in American Life*

the work of the nineteenth-century English statistician Sir Francis Galton.* In *Hereditary Genius*, published in 1869, Galton argued that intelligence ran in families.[1] Then, in the late nineteenth century, mental tests started being used to assess intelligence. In 1904 the English psychologist Charles Spearman* began using these tests to create a statistically quantifiable measure of general intellectual capacity, g.*[2] By the 1960s, there were some avid defendants of intelligence testing being used as a way of measuring underlying genetic*—inherent and inheritable—differences in mental ability. These included the American educational psychologist* Arthur Jensen,* who argued that it was futile to try to change an individual's intelligence. Jensen noted that because intelligence had a large genetic component, remedial education* programs targeting disadvantaged black schoolchildren would be ineffective at raising their IQ* (intelligence quotient) scores; the response to his article, published in the *Harvard Educational Review*, was both immediate and scathing.

The Bell Curve also addresses political issues. In 1964–5, the president of the United States, Lyndon Baines Johnson,* had introduced his "Great Society"* programs, a set of federally funded policies for reducing poverty and racial tension. They attempted to provide opportunities for those at the bottom of the class structure. But Herrnstein and Murray suggest that intelligence determines an individual's life chances. As cognitive ability cannot be changed, it places natural limitations on an individual's life chances. Their arguments challenge the wisdom of government spending in areas such as welfare.*

Overview of the Field

Modern studies of intelligence began with Charles Darwin, who stated that intelligence was a heritable*trait (a characteristic that can be passed on through the generations) and a major factor in human evolution.[3] This idea was developed by his cousin, Sir Francis Galton, who used the heritability of intelligence to explain the persistence of powerful families in Great Britain. But Galton and Darwin both lacked an accurate instrument to measure intelligence. As mental testing became more common in the nineteenth century, attempts were made to develop such an instrument. According to Herrnstein and Murray, the breakthrough was made in 1904 by the English statistician Charles Spearman, who was able to isolate what he called a "unitary mental factor" that varied consistently across mental tests. He called this factor g, for "general intelligence."

In the early twentieth century, tests measuring g were developed. These included the Stanford–Binet* test, which is still widely used today. However, in the 1960s scholars began to question whether intelligence was indeed heritable. There was a revival of scholarly interest in the psychologist B. F. Skinner's ideas about behaviorism, which suggest that humanity is malleable. The American educational psychologist Arthur Jensen rejected this, arguing that intelligence is heritable and can be correlated with educational performance. He said this is why many educational programs for struggling students— "remedial" programs—produce disappointing results.

But his was a lone voice. In the 1980s, skepticism toward g was intensified by the assertion that intelligence testing contained cultural biases against minorities. It was also undermined by the multiple intelligences* theory of the American developmental psychologist*

23

Howard Gardner,* according to which there is not one single form of intelligence; instead, intelligence expresses itself in several different ways, such as musically, linguistically, or bodily. The American evolutionary biologist Stephen Jay Gould* united these two themes in his 1981 publication, *The Mismeasure of Man*.[4]

Academic Influences

Herrnstein worked alongside the great behavioral psychologist B. F. Skinner. Despite this, the strongest academic influences on *The Bell Curve* are the work of the English statistician Charles Spearman and the American educational psychologist Arthur Jensen. Much of the *Bell Curve* is dedicated to proving their key insights—namely that:

- g (a statistically quantifiable measure of general intellectual capacity) exists and can be measured

- g is heritable and correlates with behavior such as educational achievement.

Herrnstein and Murray are also indebted to the development of regression analysis*—a statistical method used to investigate the relationship between multiple variables. The English mathematician Karl Pearson*(1857–1936) was an early advocate of using regression analysis to measure the effects of intelligence on social behavior.

The Bell Curve is a politically conservative* book. In this it owes a debt to the Anglo-Irish statesman Edmund Burke* (1729–97). Burke was a critic of revolutionary political movements and the universal Enlightenment* principles that often serve as their rationale. The Enlightenment was an intellectual movement of seventeenth- and eighteenth-century Europe that emphasized rights, liberty, and reason. Burke opposed this movement, arguing that social stability comes through incremental improvements to societies, and that these incremental improvements respect the accumulated wisdom of national cultures and political institutions. While President Johnson's* "Great Society" programs were radical rather than revolutionary, Herrnstein and Murray express Burkean skepticism towards the policies that resulted from them. These policies included an expansion of welfare and heavy investment in remedial education. The authors *of The Bell Curve* are also critical of affirmative action* programs in higher education and hiring (policies designed to increase the representation of women and minorities in areas where they have been historically underrepresented).

Those with right-wing (conservative) political views reject affirmative action on the grounds that it is an infringement of equal opportunity; opposition to this policy has become a cause célèbre—a heated issue attracting a lot of public attention—among this group.

NOTES

1   Francis Galton, *Hereditary Genius* (London: Macmillan, 1982).

2   Charles Spearman, "General Intelligence, Objectively Determined and Measured," *American Journal of Psychology* 15 (1904): 201–29.

3   Charles Darwin, *The Origin of Species* (New York: P. F. Collier & Son, 1909).

4   Stephen Jay Gould, *The Mismeasure of Man* (New York: W. W. Norton, 1981).

MODULE 3
THE PROBLEM

KEY POINTS

- *The Bell Curve* asks: Are persistent inequalities in American life due to the attributes of individual citizens or to structural causes such as unequal educational and economic opportunities?

- At the time it was published, many political scientists* and sociologists* argued that inequalities were socially derived; others argued that inequalities have a biological basis in terms of the heritability* of intelligence.

- Few scholars at the time looked to biology to explain social inequality* in such detail.

Core Question

Richard J. Herrnstein and Charles Murray's *The Bell Curve: Intelligence and Class Structure in American Life* addresses two linked questions: Is there a biological basis for the persistent inequalities in American life? And if there is, do differences in intelligence between ethnic groups* help explain the overrepresentation of minority groups* in poverty, crime, illegitimacy* (children born to unmarried parents), unemployment, and low educational achievement?

Herrnstein addressed the first question in a 1971 article he published in the American magazine *The Atlantic Monthly*, entitled "IQ."[1] In that article, and his subsequent book *IQ in the Meritocracy* (1973), Herrnstein argues that the stratification of American society is the direct result of inherited differences in cognitive ability* (something commonly understood as "intelligence"). He took a step toward answering the second question in his book *Crime and Human Nature* (1985), cowritten with Janes Q. Wilson, in which, again, he

> ❝ The egalitarian ideal of contemporary political theory underestimates the importance of the differences that separate human beings. It fails to come to grips with human variation. It overestimates the ability of political interventions to shape human character and capacities. ❞
>
> Richard J. Herrnstein and Charles Murray, *The Bell Curve: Intelligence and Class Structure in American Life*

argued that criminal behavior can also be explained in large part by hereditary factors.[2] But it was not until the publication of *The Bell Curve* that the idea of inherited *racial* differences was developed.

Murray's earlier work had also touched on ideas that were developed more fully in *The Bell Curve*. In his book *Losing Ground: American Social Policy 1950–1980* (1984), Murray argued that federal programs aiming at helping disadvantaged groups actually hurt the groups they intended to help.[3] As for which policies best aided those at the bottom of the class structure, Murray argued that America's strong tradition of civil society*(nongovernmental voluntary organizations) was more cost effective and efficacious than federal interventions. *The Bell Curve* provides the scientific rationale for this belief. It claims that environmental changes—welfare* programs to reduce poverty, remedial education* to close achievement gaps, for example—can only marginally affect an individual's life chances. Their key potentials and limitations come through cognitive ability—a trait which, being heritable, can be passed from generation to generation.

The Participants

The English statistician Sir Francis Galton* was the first person to discuss the relationship between socioeconomic status* and intelligence. Subsequent participants in the debate developed the thesis that low intelligence, a heritable and measurable trait, was linked to deviancy. In the early and mid-twentieth century this idea helped to underpin the modern eugenics* movement—the attempt to use selective breeding or sterilization to promote or reduce particular traits within a population. In a famous legal case of 1927, *Buck v. Bell*, Justice Oliver Wendell Holmes*—a judge sitting on the highest legal institution of the United States, the Supreme Court* —upheld forced sterilization for citizens of low intelligence, famously stating that "three generations of imbeciles are enough."[4] But eugenics was also championed by the extremely right-wing Nazi* regime in Germany, irreparably damaging this line of research in the eyes of many researchers.

In policy circles, the Moynihan Report* of 1965, written by the American sociologist Daniel Patrick Moynihan,* looked at problems of poverty, illegitimacy, and crime in African American communities. Moynihan argued that high rates of children born out of marriage in impoverished black communities led to poor performance in education and employment, not the other way around.[5]

But in 1969 the American psychologist Arthur Jensen* argued against this. He said intelligence, not socioeconomic status,* best predicted future achievement. Jensen was challenged on two fronts. The Harvard psychologist Howard Gardner* argued that intelligence, being multi-faceted, is not an attribute that can be defined as a singular property. Poor performance in education only tells one side of the story. Intelligence in interpersonal relationships, creativity, and bodily activities are difficult to capture in test scores, but are equally important indicators of cognitive ability.[6] In his influential book *The Mismeasure of Man* (1981), the American evolutionary biologist Stephen Jay Gould* questioned Jensen's emphasis of nature over nurture.*[7] Gould argued that intelligence has a social basis and can improve or decline depending on environmental factors.

The Contemporary Debate

Growing inequality was an established theme when *The Bell Curve* was written. The American social scientist Christopher Jencks*[8] and the American sociologist William Julius Wilson*[9] had both written classic works on the subject, each mentioned in *The Bell Curve.* Jencks and Wilson sought explanations for inequality in structural forces, such as unequal access to quality education or employment. Herrnstein and Murray entered this debate, and challenged its parameters. Rather than focusing on structural causes of inequality, they explained inequality in terms of inherited biological differences. They courted a response from the public intellectual sphere by publishing an excerpt of *The Bell Curve* in the generally liberal American magazine *The New Republic.**

Such a gesture was common in the late 1980s and early 1990s, with the American world of letters embroiled in culture wars* between liberals and conservatives, fought over such issues as abortion, education, sexuality, and religion. Herrnstein and Murray were championed by political conservatives* for stating that behaviors had a biological basis. Until *The Bell Curve,* this idea was a political taboo*— that is, it was a topic generally avoided in political discourse. In America, the grand federal policies of the twentieth century, from the building programs of President Roosevelt's New Deal* to the Great Society* of President Johnson, largely reflected the liberal consensus that behavior was determined by environmental factors and inequality was a result of social and cultural forces. Herrnstein and Murray posed a strong challenge to this political and scholarly orthodoxy (generally accepted theory).

NOTES

1 Richard J. Herrnstein, "IQ," *The Atlantic Monthly* 228 (1971): 43–64.

2 James Q. Wilson and Richard J. *Herrnstein, Crime and Human Nature* (New York: Simon and Schuster, 1985).

3 Charles Murray, *Losing Ground: American Social Policy, 1950–1980* (New York: Basic Books, 1984).

4 *Buck v. Bell*, Superintendent of State Colony Epileptics and Feeble Minded, 274 U.S. 200 (1927).

5 http://www.dol.gov/oasam/programs/history/webid-meynihan.htm, accessed October 15, 2015.

6 Howard Gardner, *Frames of Mind: The Theory of Multiple Intelligences* (New York: Basic Books, 1983).

7 Steven Jay Gould, *The Mismeasure of Man* (New York: W. W. Norton, 1981).

8 Christopher Jencks *et al.*, *Inequality: A Reassessment of the Effect of Family and Schooling in America* (New York: Basic Books, 1972).

9 William Julius Wilson, *The Truly Disadvantaged: The Inner City, the Underclass, and Public Policy* (Chicago: University of Chicago Press, 1987).

MODULE 4
THE AUTHOR'S CONTRIBUTION

KEY POINTS

- The primary aim of *The Bell Curve* is to introduce intelligence as a variable into debates concerning inequality.

- This fed into debates about the effectiveness of programs in the United States aimed at reducing gaps in education, employment, and wealth.

- *The Bell Curve* brought new levels of intensity to debates about welfare,* affirmative action,* and remedial education* programs.

Author's Aims

Geoffrey Parker has three central aims in *Global Crisis: War, Climate Change and Catastrophe in the Seventeenth Century.* The first is to bring the latest data from research into climate history to bear on the story of the General Crisis. The second is to broaden the scope of the debate on the crisis in Europe to include other regions—especially Asia. The third, as he put it in 2008, is to produce "valuable lessons for dealing with the climate challenges that undoubtedly await us and our children."[1]

Parker brings together "the climatologists' Little Ice Age* with the historian's General Crisis"[2] to see how they are related. Climate change is global even though its effects are unevenly spread. So, was the European historians' General Crisis also global? This is where Parker attempts something new. Others made forays into this area, including the anthropologist* Brian Fagan with *The Little Ice Age: How Climate Made History 1300–1850* (2000), but *Global Crisis* is the first text to bring together such a huge range of climate data to encompass the whole world ("anthropology" here refers to the study of

> ❝ Measures of intelligence have reliable statistical relationships with important social phenomena, but they are a limited tool for deciding what to make of any given individual. Repeat it we must, for one of the problems of writing about intelligence is how to remind readers often enough how little an IQ* score tells about whether the human being next to you is someone whom you will admire or cherish. This thing we know as IQ is important but not a synonym for human excellence. ❞
>
> Richard J. Herrnstein and Charles Murray, *The Bell Curve: Intelligence and Class Structure in American Life*

humankind, particularly the study of human cultural and social behavior and belief).

Approach

Parker's approach is to weave the wealth of recent data from environmental history together with older findings from political, military, cultural, social, and economic history. This hinges on having well-established work by historians in each of the more traditional fields to balance the glut of new findings from environmental and climatological historians.

On the environmental side, Parker relies on two kinds of evidence to "identify the channels by which the crisis impinges on humankind." He calls these the "natural archive" and the "human archive."[3] The former is from the natural world and is collected by climate scientists. It involves palynology:* the analysis of ice cores, and pollen and spores preserved in lakes, bogs, and other aquatic environments. There is also information from dendrochronology* (growth rings in trees) and speleothems*(the deposits from groundwater running through underground caverns). Human data includes written records, pictures, and archaeological finds. Both archives can be brought together to give a full picture of climate conditions in the past. This can then be compared with other historical data—economic, political, military, and social—to reveal the extent to which climate has affected the course of history. Since neither set of data is restricted to Europe, Parker is able to place a wider emphasis on the global scale of the crisis.

Parker is not an environmental determinist*—that is, he does not believe that climatic conditions alone determine human history. He says that to look at how extreme weather in the seventeenth century matches up with the General Crisis and blame the former for the latter would be to "paint bull's eyes around bullet holes."[4] Instead *Global Crisis* explores the links by which the climate affected societies across the globe differently, depending on their location and how resilient they were.

Contribution in Context

It is agreed that the seventeenth century was a time of unprecedented turbulence across Europe. While Parker's book is not a radical challenge to historians' ideas of what happened, it makes important contributions to three areas of study: the nature and causes of the General Crisis, the relationship between human history and climate change, and the scope of history writing.

Parker has long been a major figure in the academic world, publishing work since the 1970s. The historians of the French *Annales* School,* who particularly emphasized the role of social activity, have been notable influences on Parker's thought—Emmanuel Le Roy Ladurie* and Fernand Braudel* in particular. In this sense *Global Crisis* is a continuation of their work as well as his own. Parker is driven by insights gained from delving deep into economic and social history, and the growing number of environmental clues available at the time of writing. This shows his considerable kinship with the *Annales* approach to the past.

Parker belongs to a growing movement of historians seeking to show how important the climate is to our history and our future. During the winter of 2013–14, "hundreds of scholars attended the dozen or so panels at the annual meeting of the American Historical Association, devoted to some aspect of the impact of climate on history."[5] Parker lined up with scholars such as the American historian Julia Adney Thomas,* who argued that climate change has always been and will remain a "world-altering force."[6]

Although Parker is a specialist in European history, *Global Crisis* encourages readers to view history in a worldwide context. This springs from the need to take a global view of climate change, but is also part of a longer intellectual tradition. For Parker, it dates back to no less a figure than the eighteenth-century French philosopher and writer Voltaire,* whom he credits with being the first "global historian" and the first to identify a Global Crisis in the seventeenth century.[7]

NOTES

1   Geoffrey Parker, "Crisis and Catastrophe: The Global Crisis of the Seventeenth Century Reconsidered," *American Historical Review* 113, no. 4 (2008): 1079.

2   Geoffrey Parker, *Global Crisis: War, Climate Change and Catastrophe in the Seventeenth Century* (New Haven and London: Yale University Press, 2013), xx.

3   Parker, *Global Crisis,* xxix.

4   Parker, *Global Crisis,* xx.

5   Parker, *Global Crisis,* xvii.

6   Parker, *Global Crisis,* xvii.

7   *Historynet*, "Interview with Author-Historian Geoffrey Parker," (2013), accessed October 21, 2015, http://www.historynet.com/interview-with-author-historian-geoffrey-parker.htm.

SECTION 2
IDEAS

MODULE 5
MAIN IDEAS

KEY POINTS

- Geoffrey Parker tackles the global nature of the General Crisis* by looking at the economic, political, and social disasters that rocked the world in the seventeenth century.

- These disasters took place during a period of global cooling* that triggered extreme weather events, and Parker reveals a "fatal synergy" (interaction) between the two.

- *Global Crisis* identifies the parts of the world that were particularly vulnerable to the worst effects of the crisis, and the ones that escaped relatively unscathed.

Key Themes

In *Global Crisis: War, Climate Change and Catastrophe in the Seventeenth Century*, Geoffrey Parker describes a world so wracked by fighting, famines, and natural disasters that the great English philosopher of the day, Thomas Hobbes,* famously said that war was man's "natural state."[1]

This was not just a question of perception. The seventeenth century saw more wars and political turmoil than ever before in human history. Between 1636 and 1666, Parker counts 49 major revolts and revolutions across the world. There were 27 in Europe (including Russia and Turkey), 7 in the Americas, and 15 in Asia and Africa.[2] In several cases local conflicts triggered much longer, more widespread, more destructive wars. The Bohemian Revolt* of 1618 (an uprising in the historical Central European state of Bohemia) helped start the Thirty Years War:* "a prolonged conflict that lasted three decades and eventually involved all the major states of Europe."[3] A Manchurian* war against the Chinese emperor the same year led to 70 years of fighting in the region (Manchuria is a region forming the northeastern portion of modern China).

❝ There is no place for industry, because the fruit thereof is uncertain, and consequently, no culture of the earth; no navigation, nor use of commodities that may be imported by sea; no commodious building; no instruments of moving and removing things as require much force; no knowledge of the face of the earth; no account of time; no arts; no letters; no society. And what is worst of all, continual fear and danger of violent death; and the life of man, solitary, poor, nasty, brutish and short. ❞

Thomas Hobbes, *Leviathan*

All this took place "against a background of extreme weather events" related to global climate change.[4] Sub-Saharan Africa endured a drought from 1614 to 1619. In Europe, 1616 was known as the "year without a summer" and was the wettest in 500 years.[5] Droughts affected whole swathes of North and South America, while both Europe and the Middle East suffered intense cold during 1620.[6] Such conditions laid waste to crops and livestock, leading to widespread food shortages and famine.

These events coincided with war or rebellion so often that Parker describes a "fatal synergy" in which natural and political disasters worsened each other's effects. Where political breakdown was already occurring, infrastructure problems made the effects of crop failure worse. Elsewhere, crop failures and famine fueled political dissent and rebellion. Together, the effects added up to a "demographic,* social, and political catastrophe that lasted for two generations, and convinced contemporaries that they faced unprecedented hardship."[7]

Exploring the Ideas

Parker amassed a vast amount of evidence for marked global cooling in the seventeenth century. Daily records from an early network of observation stations "reveal that the winters between 1654 and 1667 were, on average, more than 1°C cooler than those of the later twentieth century."[8] These are supported by other scientific yardsticks for assessing climate conditions, including data from growth rings in trees as far apart as the Alps in Europe and Patagonia on the tip of South America. Taken together, the evidence gives a consistent picture of a global fall in temperature of 1°C to 2°C.[9] This was caused by an abnormally low solar activity in the early and mid-seventeenth century[10]—a decrease in the intensity of factors such as sunspots* and flares—combined with a number of major volcanic eruptions that produced high-altitude dust clouds that literally blocked out the sun.[11]

A single degree centigrade was enough to have a serious effect on growing seasons. *Global Crisis* explains how colder conditions led to catastrophic falls in crop yields across the world. The economics of the supply chain in seventeenth-century Europe meant "a 30 percent reduction in the grain harvest often *doubled* the price of bread, whereas a 50 percent reduction *quintupled* it."[12] The most densely populated areas of the early modern* world relied on a single crop: wheat or rye in Europe, rice in Asia, and maize in the Americas. Staple crops were up to 75 percent of the population's diet. These dynamics were devastating.[13]

At the same time, people around the world were enduring unprecedented levels of intense military conflict. Parker identifies the seventeenth century as the "century of the soldiers," noting that "more wars took place around the world than in any other era before the Second World War.*"[14] In Europe, the first half of the century saw "only one year entirely without war" (1610). Referencing the Ottoman Empire,* centered in what is today Turkey, and the Mughal* Empire, centered in Iran, northern India, and Pakistan, he explains that beyond Europe "the Chinese and Mughal empires fought …

continuously … and the Ottoman empire enjoyed only ten years of peace."[15] These wars were also more intense, longer, and more harmful than any in previous centuries.[16]

War caused economic and political instability as well as death and destruction. "Perhaps one million men," he writes, "served simultaneously in the various armies and navies" of Europe at huge expense to the states involved in war.[17] The creation of states where the economic needs of the military came first saw governments resorting to "a wide variety of expedients to fund their wars." They became trapped in a vicious circle of borrowing and taxation that made food shortages worse and encouraged revolution.[18]

These factors all rolled together in Parker's fatal synergy: a cycle in which climate change, political mismanagement, and war all worsened each other's effects to the point of catastrophe.

Language and Expression

Parker wrote *Global Crisis* for fellow scholars and the general public. He has an engaging style and makes reference to many literary sources alongside evidence from science and the archives. For example, evidence of the growth in literacy in Japan—which was shielded from the worst effects of the crisis—comes from the attendance figures for poetry competitions, the expansion of pornographic literature, and the popularity of tales and woodcuts representing the *ukiyo* or "floating world" of drinkers, actors, and courtesans.[19] Elsewhere, Parker's sense of humor is evident. A section on the lead role of women in many seventeenth-century protests and revolts is called "Chicks Up Front," after a common battle cry of 1960s American protesters. Then, as in the seventeenth century, the hope was that female protesters would be less likely to be beaten by police or soldiers.[20]

The use of hard scientific facts and figures sets *Global Crisis* apart from many popular history books. It is littered with tables and graphs, ranging from the average heights of "French males born between

1650 and 1770" (to show the relationship between food shortages, growth, and climatic cooling), to the locations of correspondents of the German scientist Henry Oldenburg,* and the numbers of letters he exchanged with them.[21] Though technical, such charts are always carefully explained and illustrate key points.

NOTES

1 Thomas Hobbes, *Leviathan*, ed. Richard Tuck (Cambridge: Cambridge University Press, 1996), 88.

2 Geoffrey Parker, *Global Crisis: War, Climate Change & Catastrophe in the Seventeenth Century* (New Haven and London: Yale University Press, 2013), xxii.

3 Parker, *Global Crisis*, xxvii.

4 Parker, *Global Crisis*, xxvii.

5 See John D. Post, *The Last Great Subsistence Crisis in the Western World* (Baltimore: Johns Hopkins University Press, 1977).

6 Parker, *Global Crisis*, xxvii.

7 Parker, *Global Crisis,* xxv.

8 Parker, *Global Crisis*, xx.

9 Parker, *Global Crisis*, 5.

10 Parker, *Global Crisis*, 13, 15.

11 Parker, *Global Crisis*, 13–15.

12 Parker, *Global Crisis*, 20.

13 Parker, *Global Crisis*, 19.

14 Parker, *Global Crisis,* 26.

15 Parker, *Global Crisis*, 26.

16 Parker, *Global Crisis,* 26.

17 Parker, *Global Crisis,* 32.

18 Parker, *Global Crisis,* 34.

19 Parker, *Global Crisis*, 503–4.

20 Parker, *Global Crisis*, 515 and n.

21 Parker, *Global Crisis*, 23, 659.

MODULE 6
SECONDARY IDEAS

KEY POINTS

- *Global Crisis* examines how political decisions, especially the decision to go to war, worsened the suffering caused by environmental conditions in the seventeenth century.

- Geoffrey Parker shows that these decisions stemmed from many different sources, including the rise of the court favorite (an individual particularly favored in royal circles), the belief in divine power, and the trauma of succession crises (questions over who should succeed a monarch).

- Another aggravating factor was the use of regalian (royal) rights—old, sometimes ancient, laws that allowed monarchs to do whatever they wanted.

Other Ideas

Geoffrey Parker structures *Global Crisis: War, Climate Change and Catastrophe in the Seventeenth Century* as 14 case studies. In each he focuses on a region such as Spain, England, or the Ottoman Empire* through a combination of primary historical sources and climate-change data. Parker's examination of four separate zones where "a disproportionate number of key events of the mid seventeenth century occurred"[1] helps to show the places most vulnerable to political change. Each section links back to evidence of global cooling,* such as a period of unrest in Ukraine in the seventeenth century.[2]

Parker identifies common denominators shared by many places. First, he says many rulers "claimed to embody divine power on earth, which conferred the right to make war."[3] Second, he observes that "early modern* states often experienced anarchy whenever a ruler died leaving no capable and universally recognized successor."[4] Third,

> ❝ The imposition of government initiatives by proclamations, often resurrecting or extending a 'regalian right,' enforced by royal judges with instructions to stifle any opposition within the courts, left those affected without legal redress. ❞
>
> Geoffrey Parker, *Global Crisis: War, Climate Change and Catastrophe in the Seventeenth Century*

Parker highlights the prevalence of court favorites—people who wielded huge influence over a monarch. They "abounded in the early modern world and … made war and rebellion more common."[5] Parker explains the rise of the favorite as down to the "relentless increase in the administrative burdens that weighed upon monarchs."[6]

Parker notes that these burdens led to people being robbed of traditional ways to protest. Unlike earlier times when "subjects could protest, however deferentially," these harsher administrations "brooked no challenges."[7] Here he identifies flaws within a political system that encouraged intrigue and factionalism (friction caused by the presence of factions). Rampant royal crises in Europe, however, "paled in comparison with the succession disputes that characterized some Asian dynasties."[8]

Exploring the Ideas

Parker unpicks how and why each country or region fell prey to the same sorts of problems.

An excellent example of the dangers of court favoritism was the Count-Duke of Olivares,* a man who presided over economic and social catastrophe in Iberia (present-day Spain and Portugal); he imposed new taxes through regalian rights—that is, the rights held by royalty—"which could be imposed and changed at will"[9] so easily that "government apologists ransacked historical works for justifications of their use."[10] This was deeply unpopular, notably for those taxpayers who resisted his punitive tax on salt.[11] Open revolt broke out in the Basque* region of what is today northern Spain and southern France,[12] and among certain authorities in the Catalan* region of today's northeastern Spain who refused Olivares' request to "muster 6000 troops."[13] Portugal joined in by refusing to comply when Olivares tried to raise money by "imposing the *media anata*"—in which the government kept the first year's salary of every newly appointed official.

Parker's analysis of England centers on the king's belief in divine power. The stubbornness of Charles I* led to a brutal civil war and his eventual execution. His second son, James II,* managed to stay on the throne for just three years before being forced into exile. Yet even the traumatic experience of the English Civil War* paled in comparison to the devastating effect caused by the kingly belief in the "right to rule" during the Thirty Years' War.* Simmering religious tensions and arguments about succession boiled over into a war that sucked in all the major European powers at a time when public authority in the Holy Roman Empire* (a territory encompassing modern Germany, Switzerland, Austria, and parts of Italy and the Netherlands) was divided between "1,300 territorial rulers." This catastrophic event, in which "the loss and displacement of people were proportionately greater than in [World War II*],"[14] highlighted the severely dysfunctional nature of the German political landscape.[15]

Parker takes a long look at the crisis of succession in the Ottoman Empire* that resulted in "two regicides, three depositions and significant loss of territory."[16] Here too the court favorite (the "Grand Vizier") was granted sweeping powers, but he presided over a blood-soaked court. "All male members of the Ottoman dynasty normally lived in sealed apartments in the Imperial palace appropriately known as 'the cage' (*kafes*), until one of them became Sultan and executed all the others."[17]

Parker shows that the growth of Russia "led to an equally rapid expansion of the central bureaucracy."[18] Although the seventeenth century saw the creation of 77 new government departments, access for ordinary people was severely limited. All petitions had to be addressed directly to the Tsar using "demeaning diminutives" such as "your miserable orphan."[19] As the government reached deeper into daily life, grievances and petitions multiplied."[20] The lack of any real answer to these complaints caused great unrest in Russia, as it did elsewhere.

Overlooked

Global Crisis is a relatively new text, and so serious criticism comes mostly from book reviews. The Anglo-Chilean historian and political scientist Anthony Pagden* was concerned that, although Parker demonstrated the "seventeenth century was indeed a period of crisis" and also a period of unusual and violent changes in the weather, "he had not demonstrated beyond contention that the former was caused or even precipitated by the latter."[21] Such an analysis misses Parker's fundamental point: it was the combination of "natural and human factors"[22] that fed into one another in a loop.

Another important aspect that has been overlooked is Parker's probing of the abuse of power by court favorites and monarchs. While regalian rights differed from state to state, they were always claimed by rulers who needed to raise money to fund foreign wars. Olivares's imposition of a salt tax in 1628 was a massive blunder that alienated many thousands while failing to generate enough money. Abuse of regalian rights is most commonly used in discussions of the English Civil War. Parker's understanding of this as a core cause of the crisis deserves more attention.

NOTES

1   Geoffrey Parker, *Global Crisis: War, Climate Change and Catastrophe in the Seventeenth Century* (New Haven and London: Yale University Press, 2013), xxix.

2   See Parker, *Global Crisis,* 169.

3   Parker, *Global Crisis,* 37.

4   Parker, *Global Crisis,* 45

5   Parker, *Global Crisis,* 49–50.

6   Parker, *Global Crisis,* 50.

7   Parker, *Global Crisis,* 52.

8   Parker, *Global Crisis,* 46.

9   Parker, *Global Crisis,* 257.

10 Parker, *Global Crisis,* 257.

11 Parker, *Global Crisis,* 259.

12 Parker, *Global Crisis,* 260.

13 Parker, *Global Crisis,* 263.

14 Parker, *Global Crisis,* 211.

15 Parker, *Global Crisis,* 211.

16 Parker, *Global Crisis,* 185.

17 Parker, *Global Crisis,* 190

18 Parker, *Global Crisis,* 159

19 Parker, *Global Crisis,* 159

20 Parker, *Global Crisis,* 159–60.

21 Anthony Pagden, *"Global Crisis: War, Climate Change and Catastrophe in the Seventeenth Century* by Geoffrey Parker (review)," *Common Knowledge* 21, no. 3 (2015): 515.

22 Parker, *Global Crisis,* xxv.

MODULE 7
ACHIEVEMENT

KEY POINTS

- In his earlier work Geoffrey Parker noted that global cooling* had a significant impact on the General Crisis,* but that serious investigation was hampered by a lack of evidence.

- *Global Crisis* strikes a chord with thinkers and commentators because of its relevance to the intense political debate surrounding contemporary climate change.

- Though he sounds a warning about the effects of modern-day temperature change, Parker does not go so far as to suggest that the Little Ice Age* was caused by human activity.

Assessing the Argument

Five years before the publication of *Global Crisis: War, Climate Change and Catastrophe in the Seventeenth Century,* Geoffrey Parker published an article titled "Crisis and Catastrophe," in which he argued that "the mid-seventeenth century saw more cases of simultaneous state breakdown around the globe than any previous or subsequent age."[1] As a result, "no convincing account of the General Crisis can now ignore the impact of the unique climatic conditions that prevailed."[2] The new data, he maintained, allowed the French historian Emmanuel La Roy Ladurie* to complete his *Comparative Human History of Climate* (2005) after abandoning it in 1967 for a lack of scientific evidence.[3]

Before writing *Global Crisis,* Parker realized that few historians could have studied the effect of climate on the past because "only one previous global cataclysm"—the General Crisis—had "sufficient

> **❝** Parker wants readers to take seriously the proposition
> that the various economic and political crises of the
> seventeenth century were not isolated events but
> connected. The chief connection, he maintains, is that
> they all had a component of bad weather behind them. **❞**
>
> J. R. McNeill, "Maunder Minimum and Parker Maximum"

records for [a] detailed historical study."[4] *Global Crisis*, then, was an
attempt to correct this situation, and the success of the book rests both
on Parker's reputation as a leading scholar and the strength of the
research itself. The case studies alone are valuable as an examination of
the early modern* period. When coupled with a new emphasis on the
role of climate, it is little wonder that *Global Crisis* was named the
Sunday Times "history book of the year."[5] In the first two years after
publication it was cited more than 50 times.[6]

Achievement in Context

Parker set out to show that the General Crisis of the seventeenth
century was not only a global phenomenon, but one caused by the
fatal synergy between poor political decisions and a global cooling* of
the climate. In this he was largely successful. The book was published
in 2013 and has yet to be challenged by newer research.

The controversial element of *Global Crisis* is the concept of climate
change itself. Parker faced skepticism as "vested interests and political
agents have long opposed political or regulatory action in response to
climate change by appealing to scientific uncertainty."[7] Parker made
his mission to "rewind the tape"[8] very clear. He set out to understand
catastrophes in the seventeenth century in order to predict the
consequences of climate change in the twenty-first. The political
arguments around climate tend to run along national and ideological

lines. In the United States, for example, the liberal side, following the consensus in the scientific community, "tends to ascribe it to human activity," whereas "a substantial part of the conservative side does not recognize that there is an urgent environmental question at all, and in particular that there is such a thing as man-made climate change." This American debate "manifests a more divided picture of approaches partly characterized by more radical arguments than the European discussion where there is greater unanimity about basic facts and their interpretation."[9]

The heart of the matter is whether climate change can ever be blamed on human activity. Describing the seventeenth century, Parker notes that "since the sea coal used by brewers, dyers and other manufacturers contained twice as much sulfur as that used today, its smoke darkened the air, dirtied clothes and curtains, stunted trees and flowers, blackened buildings and statues, and choked and killed the inhabitants."[10] However, this was a commentary on health consequences for the people of the 1600s and not an indication that burning fossil fuels in any way caused the Little Ice Age. Without this anthropogenic* (that is, human-caused) link, *Global Crisis* sits on the political fence. It examines the impact of climate change but avoids placing any blame on the people of the period.

Limitations

Global Crisis will stay relevant to scholars and the wider public for two reasons. First, the 14 case studies of crisis-hit regions make a serious contribution to the study of history. Second, identifying climate change as at least part of the reason for the General Crisis secures Parker a place in the ongoing debate between politicians and scientists.

Separating environmental and man-made impacts on past civilizations, however, remains difficult because of the "paucity of high-resolution paleoclimatic* evidence"—that is, the lack of evidence showing how the climate has changed throughout the earth's entire history. Regardless of the hunt for human causes for climate change in the past, the idea that it occurred at all is very important to the study of history. The Swiss climatologist Ulf Büntgen* noted that "recent warming is unprecedented"[11] but also identified two key issues. First, "increased climate variability from 250 to 600 C.E. coincided with the demise of the Western Roman Empire* and the turmoil of the Migration Period."*[12] Second, "such historical data may provide a basis for counteracting the recent political and fiscal reluctance to mitigate projected climate change."[13]

In other words, *Global Crisis* reaches beyond understanding the effects of global cooling on the seventeenth century and into the present day. Though not the first such analysis, it is by far the most ambitious, with the notable exception of Ladurie's three-volume work on climate change that took even longer to write than the 15 years Parker devoted to *Global Crisis*. Parker's text looks set to serve as a template for further research into the effect of climate on history.

NOTES

1   Geoffrey Parker, "Crisis and Catastrophe: The Global Crisis of the Seventeenth Century Reconsidered," *American Historical Review* 113, no. 4 (2008): 1053.

2   Parker, "Crisis and Catastrophe," 1077.

3   Parker, "Crisis and Catastrophe," 1077.

4   Parker, "Crisis and Catastrophe," 1077.

5   Parker, "Crisis and Catastrophe," 1079.

6   Google Scholar, "Parker Global Crisis," accessed September 29, 2015, https://scholar.google.com/scholar?hl=en&q=Parker+Global+Crisis&btnG=&as_sdt=1%2C9&as_sdtp=.

7   Stephan Lewandowsky et al., "Seepage: Climate Change Denial and Its Effect on the Scientific Community," *Global Environmental Change* 33 (2015): 1.

8   Geoffrey Parker, *Global Crisis: War, Climate Change and Catastrophe in the Seventeenth Century* (New Haven and London: Yale University Press, 2013), xix.

9   Roland Benedikter et al., "The 'American Way of Life' and US Views on Climate Change and the Environment," in *Cultural Dynamics of Climate Change and the Environment in North America*, ed. Bernd Sommer (Leiden, Netherlands: Brill Publishing, 2015), 22.

10   Parker, *Global Crisis*, 61.

11   Ulf Büntgen et al., "2500 Years of European Climate Variability and Human Susceptibility," *Science* 331, no. 6017 (2011): 578.

12   Büntgen, "2500 Years," 578.

13   Büntgen, "2500 Years," 578.

MODULE 8
PLACE IN THE AUTHOR'S WORK

KEY POINTS

- Geoffrey Parker was a distinguished military historian before turning his attention to the catastrophic effects of climate on human affairs in 1997.

- During a long career, Parker has returned time and again to explaining the dramatic events of the sixteenth and seventeenth centuries, especially in Europe.

- *Global Crisis* was published amid an increasingly urgent worldwide debate about climate change and offered the possibility that lessons from the past might help make policy for the future.

Positioning

Geoffrey Parker's *Global Crisis: War, Climate Change and Catastrophe in the Seventeenth Century* stands out as something of a departure from his usual work. Previously, his main interest had been the military history of Europe between 1500 and 1700, especially of the Spanish Empire. Parker's work on warfare in the General Crisis dates back more than 30 years and includes *The Dutch Revolt* (1977), *Europe in Crisis, 1598–1648* (1979) and *The Thirty Years' War (1984)*. But his contribution as a historian also stretches beyond this period. His 1988 book *The Military Revolution: Military Innovation and the Rise of the West, 1500–1800* is regarded as a hugely important work. He is also the author of *The Times Concise History of the World* and *The Times Compact Atlas of World History* (the fifth edition of which was published in 2008).[1] Parker's work began with an interest in a specific period, then became focused on the complex causes and events of the General Crisis.

Although Parker began talking about a possible link between

> ❝ Parker vigorously argues that this climate turn destabilized many societies, especially in Eurasia. The typical litany of misfortunes involved (in approximately this chronological order, but with overlaps and variations) harvest failures, soaring food prices, famine, demographic crisis, economic crisis, popular revolt, fiscal crisis, and war—war and more war, which often compounded famines and demographic, economic, and fiscal crises in a grim negative feedback loop. ❞
>
> J. R. McNeill, *Maunder Minimum and Parker Maximum*

climate change and political disaster in his 1978 work *The General Crisis of the Seventeenth Century*, it did not become the main focus of his work until the 2008 article "Crisis and Catastrophe," in which he noted that "throughout the Northern Hemisphere, the mid-seventeenth century witnessed almost unprecedented human mortality." Indeed, "the frequency of popular revolts around the world ... peaked" during this time, the level of which would not be seen again around the world until the 1940s. More significantly, "only a few of those who lived through the seventeenth century crisis linked the catastrophes that surrounded them with climate change."[2]

Integration

A definite theme runs through Parker's long career as a historian. Time and again he grapples with how to explain the extraordinary events that shook the seventeenth-century world. The central thrust of *The Military Revolution* is Parker's assertion that advances in military technology allowed Europeans to create the world's first truly global empires. The use of gunpowder weapons in the 1500s had been perfected by the 1600s, and they were used to forge empires from the 1700s. Here are the roots of the General Crisis. In *The Thirty Years War*,

Parker explores a key conflict in the entire crisis, when people had to live with the "uncertainties and horrors of the longest, most expensive and brutal war that had yet been fought on German soil."[3]

In 2004, Parker looked again at the sixteenth- and seventeenth-century Netherlands in the second edition of *The Dutch Revolt*. He pored over the practical planning involved in the conflict between Spain and its Dutch possessions, and explored the onset of problems in the sixteenth century and the ramifications felt later in the General Crisis. A meticulous study of historical figures such as the Count-Duke of Olivares,* who "paid no attention to the opinion of others,"[4] lends weight to the idea that Parker's writing can be seen as a single, if loosely connected, body of work. The only deviations from the common thread are projects such as *The Times Compact Atlas of World History*.

Parker spelled out his interest in climate change as an important element of the General Crisis in his 2008 article "Crisis and Catastrophe." New work by climatologists made it possible to "recreate detailed weather maps for western Europe back to 1659 by month and 1500 by season."[5] Parker was quick to point out that although these offered a "detailed reconstruction of both the European climate between 1675 and 1715 and the entire global crisis for certain decades of the early modern* period,"[6] it did not show the whole picture. There was still no study of the entire seventeenth-century world despite, as Parker noted, the abundant natural and human archive revealing "extreme cold and drought around the globe."[7] Crucially, no survey had "yet appeared for the 1640s, the decade at the center of the General Crisis."[8]

Significance

Global Crisis is an ambitious attempt to plug gaping holes in our knowledge of climate change and politics during a tumultuous era. To do this Parker had to venture into a relatively new field. The effect of climate on the course of history is important to our understanding of the past, especially when historians find themselves embroiled in political debates about the effect of climate in the present. Parker was not the only one to take a closer look at the impact of extreme weather on our ancestors, and other scholars pay tribute to his work. The American historian John L. Brooke's *Climate Change and the Course of Human History* (2014) acknowledged that Parker "developed interpretations of the seventeenth century crisis solidly grounded in ecological circumstances," and "decisively altered the equation with the first definitive analysis of the impact of the Little Ice Age* on the seventeenth century."[9]

The potential for *Global Crisis* to represent a "tipping point" remains strong. As another American, the historian and anthropologist* Joseph A. Tainter* pointed out in 2000, "the historical sciences in particular are given little consideration in the making of contemporary decisions."[10] Tainter's belief that "historical research should be included in policy decisions as routinely as the findings of climatologists"[11] has not yet come to pass. However, the idea that historical research is relevant to contemporary policy decisions has been energized by the publication of *Global Crisis*. Parker's epic study remains a deeply influential work that builds on our understanding of the General Crisis and extends the debate to our own era.

NOTES

1 Ohio State University (OSU), Department of History, "Geoffrey Parker," accessed September 3, 2015, http://history.osu.edu/directory/parker277.

2 Geoffrey Parker, "Crisis and Catastrophe: The Global Crisis of the Seventeenth Century Reconsidered," *American Historical Review* 113, no. 4 (2008): 1053, 1056.

3 Christopher R. Fredrichs, "The War in Myth, Legend and History," in *The Thirty Years War,* ed. Geoffrey Parker, 2nd edn (New York: Routledge, 1997), 181.

4   Geoffrey Parker, *The Army of Flanders and the Spanish Road 1567–1659*, 2nd edn (Cambridge: Cambridge University Press, 2004), 220.

5   Geoffrey Parker, "Crisis and Catastrophe," 1066.

6   Geoffrey Parker, "Crisis and Catastrophe," 1066.

7   Geoffrey Parker, "Crisis and Catastrophe," 1066–7.

8   Geoffrey Parker, "Crisis and Catastrophe," 1066–7.

9   John L. Brooke, *Climate Change and the Course of Global History: A Rough Journey* (New York: Cambridge University Press, 2014), 450.

10 Joseph A. Tainter, "Global Change, History and Sustainability," in *The Way the Wind Blows: Climate History, and Human Action*, ed. Roderick J. McIntosh et al. (New York: Columbia University Press, 2000), 131.

11 Tainter, "Global Change," 131.

SECTION 3
IMPACT

MODULE 9
THE FIRST RESPONSES

KEY POINTS

- Early critics of *Global Crisis* suggested that Europe received too much attention and other parts of the world too little.
- Others questioned Geoffrey Parker's claim that Japan had escaped the worst of the Little Ice Age.*
- After spending 15 years researching and writing his ambitious book, Parker decided against making any changes in response to criticism.

Criticism

Early critics were often unable to separate the seventeenth-century climate change discussed by Geoffrey Parker in *Global Crisis: War, Climate Change and Catastrophe in the Seventeenth Century* from twenty-first century rows about the environment.

The US historian Markus Vink* said that Parker "makes not only a powerful case for the role of climate change in inducing crises in human history but also a blistering attack against the prevailing 'culture of denial' regarding global warming."[1] This fails to recognize that, unlike the debate around modern-day global warming,* Parker's discussion of past global cooling* does not suggest any human cause. His book only helps the modern debate in one way—by demonstrating the catastrophic effects of climate change, whatever the cause.

The publication of the paperback gave Parker a chance to answer some of his critics, including Jack Goldstone,* a US sociologist* and political scientist who pointed to a number of questions that *Global Crisis* did not address, including "why the scientific revolution succeeded in Europe"[2] and why China did not capitalize on late seventeenth-century trade gains.[3]

> **"** We can now be sufficiently precise about at least some past weather events that we can tie them to the sorts of political and social events that unfold in months and years, not just the more diffuse patterns of decades or centuries. This allows us to write histories in which both relatively large patterns of climate and specific human decisions matter, in a way that was not possible when *Annales** historians pioneered discussions of climate and history more than thirty years ago. **"**
>
> Kenneth Pomeranz, *Weather, War, and Welfare*

Kenneth Pomeranz,* an American expert in Chinese history, criticized Parker's analysis of early Tokugawa Japan.* According to Parker, "the Japanese archipelago has always been extremely vulnerable to climate change,"[4] and therefore "could not escape the effects of the Little Ice Age."[5] Pomeranz called *Global Crisis* "one of the most important history books of the last year,"[6] but felt "the book is still about Europe more than anywhere else ... in part because it is focused on instances of state breakdown, and Europe simply had more states per population to break down than did Asia."[7] Parker's data showed a significant increase in Japan's population, concluding that "the differences between Japan and elsewhere thus seem less impressive than Parker suggests, and the links between prudent policy and economic success much murkier."[8]

The American environmental historian* J. R. McNeill* also heaped praise upon the text while wondering if it was truly global or neglected some parts of the world. He described Parker as "decidedly Eurasia centric, perhaps even Eurocentric* and within that perhaps Britannia centric."[9] He highlighted that of the 12 main chapters "one of each is devoted to China, Japan and India, Indonesia and Iran share one chapter. One alone is devoted to all of the Americas, Africa and

Australia. Seven deal with various parts of Europe and another on the Ottoman Empire* which straddles Europe and Asia. The British Isles gets two chapters."[10]

Responses

Parker answered these criticisms by saying there was not enough space to write a complete history of the General Crisis, especially when he was restricted to the sources available.[11] He acknowledges that "although the human and natural archives from the mid-seventeenth century are abundant, they relate overwhelmingly to only two continents, Europe and Asia."[12] The historical record of Africa, the Americas and Australia is limited, making it virtually impossible to examine these regions with a high degree of academic rigor. He tended to focus on places with the best records, so Europe and Asia attracted more attention.

Parker also tackled Pomeranz's question about whether Japan had indeed "escaped the full rigor of the Little Ice Age—and, if so, how."[13] Referencing the seventeenth-century military leader Tokugawa Iemitsu,* Parker wrote, "Perhaps *Global Crisis* did not make sufficiently clear that I regard major political change, like that of early modern* Japan, as a prolonged and complex process. The central government did not suddenly implement a single successful policy to mitigate the impact of climate change; rather, it took a series of initiatives that, taken together, promoted peace and prosperity, and it encouraged regional authorities to follow suit. Thus, by the time the Little Ice Age occurred, the legislation of Tokugawa Iemitsu in the 1640s ... for the most part normalized policies already in place for two and even three generations." The links between prudent policy and economic success "postulated in *Global Crisis*," he added, "thus remain intact."[14]

Conflict and Consensus

Parker agreed his critics had raised fascinating and important questions but was conscious of how much longer the book would need to be to address them. He decided to "merely correct some errors noted by my erudite colleagues."[15] Parker takes some time to repeat his response to Pomeranz but this is mostly in the preface to the paperback edition of *Global Crisis*. He does not change the main text in answer to any criticism and the reasons for this seem clear. As Goldstone noted, "Parker invested fifteen years in preparing this book and it shows."[16] Although Parker "resisted the temptation to scour the world's archives he seems otherwise to have allowed his curiosity free reign."[17]

It seems that in Parker's mind the work is complete, and he appears to have deliberately avoided any attempt to take on his critics. Parker is clearly no climate-change skeptic and does not choose to address anyone who disputes whether human activity can affect the environment. He has "produced his most comprehensive work to date, a truly global history of the seventeenth century that embraces Europe, Africa, the Middle East, Russia, China, Japan, India, Southeast Asia, and even Australia and the Americas with great skill and immense scholarship."[18]

NOTES

1   Markus Vink, "Review: *Global Crisis: War, Climate Change and Catasatrophe in the Seventeenth Century* by Geoffrey Parker," *Journal of Modern History* 86, no. 3 (2014): 640.

2   Jack A. Goldstone, " Climate Lessons from History," *Historically Speaking* 14, no. 5 (2013): 37.

3   Goldstone, "Climate Lessons from History," 37.

4   Geoffrey Parker, *Global Crisis: War, Climate Change and Catastrophe in the Seventeenth Century* (New Haven and London: Yale University Press, 2013), 485.

5   Parker, *Global Crisis,* 485.

6   Kenneth Pomeranz, "Weather, War, and Welfare: Persistence and Change in Geoffrey Parker's *Global Crisis,*" *Historically Speaking* 14, no. 5 (2013): 30.

7   Pomeranz, "Weather, War, and Welfare," 30.

8   Pomeranz, "Weather, War, and Welfare," 30.

9   J. R. McNeill, "Maunder Minimum and Parker Maximum," *Historically Speaking* 14, no. 5 (2013): 34.

10 McNeill, "Maunder Minimum and Parker Maximum," 34.

11 Parker, *Global Crisis,* xv.

12 Parker, *Global Crisis,* 445.

13 Parker, "Response," *Historically Speaking* 14, no. 5 (2013), 38.

14 Parker, "Response," 38.

15 Parker, *Global Crisis*, xv.

16 Goldstone " Climate Lessons from History," 37.

17 Goldstone " Climate Lessons from History," 37.

18 Goldstone " Climate Lessons from History," 35.

MODULE 10
THE EVOLVING DEBATE

KEY POINTS

- Geoffrey Parker's ideas lend urgency to the debate about climate change and what it might mean for people around the world.

- While *Global Crisis* is too recent to be responsible for a school of thought, there are signs one could emerge from the application of his methods to other periods of history.

- Seventeenth-century upheavals coincided with the scientific revolution and provided Parker with a wealth of data; other eras are not so rich in source material but can still be studied for links between the weather and war.

Uses and Problems

While Geoffrey Parker was not the first to link weather chaos with historical events, *Global Crisis: War, Climate Change and Catastrophe in the Seventeenth Century* drew more attention than any other book on the subject. Parker's reputation as a highly influential and respected historian guaranteed a place for climate change in the international spotlight. Since the book appeared in 2013, other scholars have joined Parker in investigating the subject. The Japanese scientist Aono Yasayuki* studied cherry blossoms to identify the temperatures in Tokyo during the Tokugawa* period (1602–1868). Her research confirmed Parker's identification of a cold period in "the second half of the seventeenth century."[1] Another example of the text's wide-reaching influence is the work of the Irish economist Morgan Kelly.* He agreed with the general thrust of Parker's argument, stating that "the supposed ramifications of the Little Ice Age* … reach far beyond meteorology into economic, political, and cultural history."[2]

> ❝ Parker's analysis demonstrates the 'synchronicity, the interdependence and the interactions of the various revolutions' by taking into account the role played by contingency. For Parker, nothing is ever quite inevitable. ❞
>
> Mary Lindemann, "Review: *Global Crisis: War, Climate Change and Catastrophe in the Seventeenth Century*"

This suggests broad agreement in the academic world about the text's importance. As the American historian Mary Lindemann* points out, Parker's book existed in "a scholarly world often populated by Lilliputian* [that is, very small] studies based on thin documentation." *Global Crisis* "presents a simple yet forceful argument about the character of the seventeenth century."[3] Whether or not it is Parker's most important work remains to be seen, but interest in historical climate change shows no sign of slowing down.

Schools of Thought

Since *Global Crisis* was only published a few years ago, there has not been time for a school of thought to emerge. Parker relies heavily on an existing set of ideas generally known as the General Crisis* debate. As he says, "historians have christened this age of turmoil 'the General Crisis' and some have seen it as the gateway to the modern world."[4] This gateway idea has been established for a long time, and even Parker's expansion of the crises into something "truly global," where "no place, or virtually none, remained untouched,"[5] is not radical enough to be considered a new school of thought.

Parker's foray into climate science cannot be said to be a radical departure, either. Climatologists (scholars of climate) have to compare their findings against past records in order to determine trends in the weather, and climatology has evolved as a discipline as new techniques emerge. Just a few decades ago, for example, the notion of using ice cores to determine carbon dioxide levels over time would have been considered ridiculous; today this is accepted as an effective technique. By including such new findings, Parker adds a level of authority to his work that previous studies lacked. As time passes and techniques improve, it is possible that a school of thought could emerge based on applying Parker's methods to other periods of history.

In Current Scholarship

The ideas in *Global Crisis* do not belong to historians alone, being valuable to those locked in debate over climate change who want to understand how "the author weaves climatic and structural forces together with human actions."[6] Parker's theories are not limited to the seventeenth century. They serve as a road map for the possible consequences of man-made climate change now and in the future.

Parker's field of study is not as relevant to all areas of historical inquiry, however. The onset of the Little Ice Age coincided with the beginnings of the scientific revolution. While data on climate change reaches back into pre-history, the wealth of sources available for Parker to draw on in *Global Crisis* does not exist for earlier periods since "as regards the physical science … solid progress had to wait upon the instrumental breakthroughs (telescope, barometer, thermometer, chronometer…) between 1600 and 1750."[7] (A barometer is an instrument that measures atmospheric pressure; a chronometer measures time.)

Other eras in history, however, do meet Parker's criteria for what he describes as a "fatal synergy." Recent studies manage to combine historical data with modern scientific methods that can examine past climate change. The Israeli geography professor Ronnie Ellenblum* tells the story of well-documented climatic disasters that altered the face of the eastern Mediterranean.[8] By examining the effect of recurring droughts and famines on Egypt and other Mediterranean civilizations during the tenth and eleventh centuries, Ellenblum illustrates the role climate played in the decline of some of the region's most important civilizations.

The American geophysicist Neville Brown's* *History and Climate Change: A Eurocentric* Perspective* highlights the significance of rainfall cycles on human life. Brown links long dry spells to the rise of Genghis Khan,*[9] the powerful Mongolian emperor of the twelfth century.

The climatologist J. R. Fleming's* work on climate change provides "historical perspectives on climate and climatic changes from the Enlightenment to the late-twentieth century," and acknowledges that "great uncertainties exist in our scientific knowledge of the Earth system, and there is much to be learned about clouds, the oceans, the biosphere, geochemical cycles, and other processes. Human behavior is also quite varied and represents a real 'wild card' in the Earth system." This wild card, he says, "has not received adequate attention."[10]

NOTES

1   Aono Yasayuki, "Cherry Blossom Phenological Data since the Seventeenth Century for Edo (Tokyo), Japan, and Their Application to Estimation of March Temperatures," *International Journal of Biometeorology* 59, no. 4 (2015): 427.

2   Morgan Kelly and Cormac Ó Gráda, "The Waning of the Little Ice Age: Climate Change in Early Modern Europe," *Journal of Interdisciplinary History* 44, no. 3 (2014): 301–25.

3   Mary Lindemann, "*Global Crisis: War, Climate Change and Catastrophe in the Seventeenth Century* by Geoffrey Parker," *German Studies Review* 38, no. 1 (2015): 157.

4   Geoffrey Parker, *Global Crisis War, Climate Change and Catastrophe in the Seventeenth Century* (New Haven and London: Yale University Press, 2013), xx.

5   Lindemann, "*Global Crisis*," 157.

6   Lindemann, "*Global Crisis*," 157.

7   Neville Brown, *History and Climate Change: A Eurocentric Perspective* (New York: Routledge, 2014), 22.

8   Ronnie Ellenblum, *The Collapse of the Eastern Mediterranean: Climate Change and the Decline of the East, 950–1072* (Cambridge: Cambridge University Press, 2012), 1.

9   Brown, *History and Climate Change*, 24.

10 James Rodger Fleming, *Historical Perspectives on Climate Change* (New York and Oxford: Oxford University Press, 1998), vii.

MODULE 11
IMPACT AND INFLUENCE TODAY

KEY POINTS

- If the intensifying climate change* debate has the potential to damage the credibility of Geoffrey Parker's claims, his purely historical work represents another stage in a distinguished career.

- Regardless of how campaigners and politicians choose to use *Global Crisis*, the text has highlighted the importance of climate change on historical events and cannot be easily dismissed.

- Advances in scientific knowledge about the earth's weather throughout history allow scholars to link an increasing number of human events to climate change.

Position

It is hard to judge the impact of Geoffrey Parker's *Global Crisis: War, Climate Change and Catastrophe in the Seventeenth Century* since it involves not just historians, but everyone engaged in the intense climate change debate. On the one hand, *Global Crisis* illustrates the dramatic effect the climate can have upon the world's population, regardless of the links Parker makes to the fatal interaction between climate and political decisions. On the other, Parker does not claim that global cooling* was the result of human action. This removes one of the key sticking points of the contemporary debate—whether global warming is man-made.

The Australian psychologist Stephan Lewandowsky* observed that "opponents of the scientific consensus on climate change ... have often emphasized scientific uncertainty in order to forestall mitigative action"[1]—that is, climate-change deniers throw doubt on the science

> ❝ Geoffrey Parker's *Global Crisis* represents a coming of age for the increasingly dynamic study of past climate change and its human consequences. Such 'climate history' has a proud academic lineage, but it has long lingered in the margins of serious historical study. With *Global Crisis,* Parker, among the most eminent historians of the early modern* period, brings climate change into the mainstream of his profession. And not a moment too soon, for past relationships between humans and climate change can inform how we adapt to climate change today. ❞
>
> Dagomar Degroot, "Review: *Global Crisis: Climate Change and Catastrophe in the Seventeenth Century*"

to put off making changes to relieve its effects. Although Parker's techniques are no less subject to scientific uncertainty than any others, the issue becomes tangled up with politics. As "political decisions inevitably involve options with uncertain outcomes,"[2] all options contain unknown probabilities, such as what effect they might have on the economy.

Meanwhile, the impact of Parker's historical analysis remains strong, and his case studies follow the narrative approach to history by connecting the stories of the past. As the US sociologist* Jack Goldstone* points out, *Global Crisis* is a continuation of Parker's earlier "outstanding studies of how Spain financed its armies in the Netherlands and of the administration of Philip II,* making key contributions to our conceptualization of the 'Fiscal State' in early modern Europe." ("Fiscal State" refers to a system in which economic matters define the nature and functioning of the state.) Having established his reputation, Parker "then produced definitive studies of the general crisis of the seventeenth century, which served as an inspiration to a generation of world historians," and "followed these with enormously innovative accounts of warfare and military technique, spawning an important debate on the 'Military Revolution' in the rise of the West."[3] With such achievements already behind him, the positioning of *Global Crisis* as a work of immense importance is assured.

Interaction

As far back as 2004—a decade before *Global Crisis* appeared—the American science historian Naomi Oreskes* was lamenting that "policymakers and the media, particularly in the United States, frequently assert that climate science is highly uncertain. Some have used this as an argument against adopting strong measures to reduce greenhouse gas emissions."[4] It was against such a background that Parker published *Global Crisis*, acknowledging his text was unusual by saying "few historians include the weather in their analysis."[5]

The highly uncertain nature of climate change stems from projections about the future, not analysis of the past where, according to the geophysicist Neville Brown,* "it has long been appreciated that, in relation to the temperature life forms tolerate, the climate of our planet has been remarkably uniform."[6] However, "viewed more closely it is constantly inconsistent," and a growing awareness of what this means could give "historical climatology wider currency."[7]

As Brown points out, this way of thinking lies at the heart of how people react to *Global Crisis*. Since "before the expansion of coal production began 250 years ago, the balance was heavily towards climate cause and human consequence," analysis of the past can only yield results on the effects of climate, not the effect of human action upon it. A contrast has emerged, however, between "then" and "now." Before the Industrial Age,* which from the end of the eighteenth century has seen a move away from agricultural to industrial economies with important social consequences, "climate improvement meant warming in most European minds." Modern minds see it differently because, although a warmer climate caused less stress for the elderly and children, it also "signified [an integrated] adjustment involving sunshine, wind and—above all—rainfall." Changes in rainfall and disrupted wind patterns might also affect the spread of disease.[8]

For all these reasons the examination of climate's effect on historical events is far from over. The work of writers and researchers will inevitably be sucked into the more general global-warming debate of the present, but their true mission is to explain the past. Climate, as Parker has demonstrated, has had an enormous impact upon historical events. Further research is now needed into other specific eras in order to fully develop a new school of thought.

The Continuing Debate

The debate on the effect of dramatic shifts in the weather on our history shows no signs of abating. Since at least 1917 historians have been interested in how the climate affected events, such as the fall of the Western Roman Empire* more than 1,500 years ago.[9] The way modern scientific data is used in, for example, Neville Brown's *History and Climate Change* leads to a more complete picture. Warlike behavior during Classical times coincided with "a 12–14 year drought cycle that emerges, raggedly but insistently, from a graph of rainfall in the [Soviet Union*] from 1890 to 1970."[10] In 406 C.E. the Germanic tribe the Vandals* were able to cross the frozen Rhine river and "ten to thirteen years later … a huge tribute was extracted from Constantinople."*[11] These traumatic events can be linked to the same weather cycle, as revealed by the meticulous work of Soviet climate researchers centuries later. Future research may well reveal even deeper connections between climate and historical crisis.

Even without data from the time in question, it might be possible to identify climate changes that match historical events. An increased understanding of the solar magnetic activity cycle, for example, means we know it is set at an almost uniform 11 years from maximum to minimum. Such knowledge allows researchers to work out how much solar radiation earth received, even without sunspot* data. El Niño* (a cycle of currents in the Pacific Ocean) is less predictable than the sun but is still a natural phenomenon with a rhythm. New scientific information allows human history to be subjected to climate analysis, but only through painstaking research.

NOTES

1   Stephan Lewandowsky et al., "Seepage: Climate Change Denial and Its Effect on the Scientific Community," *Global Environmental Change* 33 (July 2015): 1.

2   Lewandowsky, "Seepage," 2.

3   Jack A. Goldstone, "Climate Lessons from History," *Historically Speaking* 14, no. 5 (2013): 37.

4   Naomi Oreskes, "Beyond the Ivory Tower: The Scientific Consensus on Climate Change," *Science* 306, no. 5702 (2004): 1686.

5   Geoffrey Parker, *Global Crisis: War, Climate Change and Catastrophe in the Seventeenth Century* (New Haven and London: Yale University Press, 2013), xviii.

6   Neville Brown, *History and Climate Change: A Eurocentric Perspective* (New York: Routledge, 2014), 3.

7   Brown, *History and Climate Change*, 3.

8   Brown, *History and Climate Change*, 3.

9   See Ellsworth Huntington, "Climate Change and Agricultural Exhaustion as Elements in the Fall of Rome," *Quarterly Journal of Economics* 33, no. 2 (1917): 173–208.

10 Brown, *History and Climate Change*, 3.

11 Brown, *History and Climate Change*, 3.

MODULE 12
WHERE NEXT?

KEY POINTS

- Geoffrey Parker's high profile and great standing in the academic world have attracted more attention to the field of climate change* history and inspired scholars to find out how the weather weaves into the human story.

- As more scientists and historians seek to understand how climate affects our past and our future, *Global Crisis* stands as a challenge to further increase our knowledge.

- Though only published in 2013, *Global Crisis* is already considered a seminal investigation into the General Crisis* of the seventeenth century.

Potential

Geoffrey Parker achieves two main objectives with *Global Crisis: War, Climate Change and Catastrophe in the Seventeenth Century*. First, he argues convincingly that what historians of European history have termed the General Crisis of the seventeenth century was a worldwide phenomenon, affected by climate change. Second, he has brought the idea of climate history back into the public's consciousness by writing a hugely successful book. Although difficulties exist in extending a "fatal synergy" between politics and climate change to other periods in time, Parker has planted the idea firmly in the public mind.[1] As the American historian Mary Lindemann* observed, even though "Parker views this crisis as historically unique," climate change itself has certainly been a factor in human history.[2]

Parker's text also serves as a reminder that debate on the General Crisis continues. By expanding the crisis to cover the entire globe, Parker takes the discussion into controversial new areas; his opini

NOTES

1   Geoffrey Parker, *Global Crisis: War, Climate Change and Catastrophe in the Seventeenth Century* (New Haven and London: Yale University Press, 2013), xxv.

2   Mary Lindemann, "*Global Crisis: War, Climate Change and Catastrophe in the Seventeenth Century* by Geoffrey Parker," *German Studies Review* 38, no. 1 (2015): 157.

3   Jack A. Goldstone, "Climate Lessons from History," *Historically Speaking* 14, no. 5 (2013): 37.

4   Dagomar Degroot, "Review: *Global Crisis: War Climate Change and Catastrophe in the Seventeenth Century,*" *E-International Relations*, http://www.e-ir.info/2014/12/12/review-global-crisis-war-climate-change-catastrophe-in-the-17th-century, accessed October 6, 2015.

5   Unpublished at the time of writing, see: http://explore.georgetown.edu/researchprojects/82290/.

6   Kenneth Pomeranz, "Weather, War, and Welfare: Persistence and Change in Geoffrey Parker's *Global Crisis,*" *Historically Speaking* 14, no. 5 (2013): 30.

7   J. R. McNeil, "Maunder Minimum and Parker Maximum," *Historically Speaking* 14, no. 5 (2013): 3.

8   Goldstone, "Climate Lessons from History," 37.

9   Pomeranz, "Weather, War, and Welfare," 30.

10 Pomeranz, "Weather, War, and Welfare," 30.

GLOSSARY

GLOSSARY OF TERMS

Annales School: a school of thought in the discipline of history that places social activity, as opposed to political or economic factors, at the center of historical study. Lucien Febvre and Marc Bloch founded the school while they taught at Strasburg University in the late 1920s.

Anthropogenic: something caused by human activity.

Anthropology: the study of humankind, particularly human belief, culture, and society.

Basque: relating to the culture, people, and language of the Basque people of southern France and northern Spain.

Bohemian Revolt: an uprising in the historical state of Bohemia, largely encompassed by the present-day Czech Republic, that took place between 1618 and 1620, provoked by Christian sectarian interests in the successor of Emperor Matthias, the state's heirless ruler.

Capitalism: an economic system whereby institutions are regulated by the laws of supply and demand. It tends toward a free-market model in which people are allowed to buy and sell goods without too much interference from governments.

Catalan: related to the language, culture, and people of Catalonia, a region in the northeast of Spain.

Climate change: a change in weather patterns over a protracted period of time. The nature of climate change is that temperature fluctuation of as little as one degree can have dramatic consequences for the planet.

Cold War: a period of great tension between the United States and the Soviet Union, and their respective allies; the Cold War lasted from around 1945 to 1991.

Communism: a political and ideological movement based on the teachings of Karl Marx. The term has its origins in the word "communist," which Karl Marx used to describe his concept of a perfect state.

Constantinople: a city in modern Turkey that takes its name from the Roman Emperor Constantine who, in 320 C.E., declared what was once the capital of the Byzantine empire to be the new capital of the Roman Empire.

Counter Reformation: a response to the Reformation and an attempt to reform the Church along less radical grounds than those proposed by Martin Luther.

Cultural turn: a movement in the humanities from the early 1970s onwards. In the practice of history, this meant a move from purely political or economic histories, to histories also concerned with the way language works, and how cultural artifacts such as objects or novels might also be used to write history.

Defenestration: the act of throwing someone out of the window. The term was coined around the time of what remains perhaps the most famous defenestration of all time—the second defenestration of Prague in 1618, in which three Catholics miraculously survived being thrown from the third floor of the Bohemian Chancellery. This act precipitated the Thirty Years War.

Demographics: the study of the structure of specific populations, commonly expressed statistically and measuring things such as age, religion, ethnicity, and so on.

Dendrochronology: the science of studying tree rings in order to determine the dates and chronological order of events in the past.

Determinism: the idea that for every event that occurs there is a root cause that could not have created any other outcome.

Early modern period: a period of European history that took place roughly between the late fifteenth and the late eighteenth centuries.

El Niño: a cyclic change in the temperature of currents emanating from the Pacific Ocean.

English Civil War: a series of armed conflicts that took place between 1642 and 1651. The battles took place between supporters of the rights of Parliament and supporters of the rights of the king, then Charles I. The parliamentarian forces won the war.

Environmental history: study of the climate in past times, and of the impact of human action on the environment.

Eurocentric: placing emphasis on the importance of European events.

Feudalism: a political system that existed from around the ninth century to the fifteenth century. Society was structured so that lords would "loan" the use of land to vassals in return for loyalty and service.

French Revolution (1789–99): a period of political and social upheaval with considerable repercussions for European history, that culminated in the execution of the French king, Louis XVI, and the drafting of several transitory constitutions.

General Crisis: a term first popularized by historian Hugh Trevor-Roper that refers to the numerous hardships suffered by the people of the mid-seventeenth century all over the world. The term generally refers to political and man-made disasters only.

Global cooling: a cooling of mean temperatures across the entire earth caused by a number of factors, including a significant decrease in solar activity. The seventeenth century experienced a particularly cold spell that began in 1650.

Global warming: a period of gradual increase in the temperature of the earth's land and oceans.

Historiography: the study of the methodology historians employ, and its development as an academic discipline.

Holocene: this era began some 11,700 years ago and continues to this day. It consists of a warm or interglacial period that exists in the middle of an ice age. All written human history and the rise of all great civilizations have occurred within this period.

Holy Roman Empire: a loose confederation of states that covered most of modern Germany and significant portions of central Europe. Established during the early Middle Ages, it was finally dissolved by the French emperor Napoleon in 1806.

Industrial Age: an era that began in England during the mid-eighteenth century and saw a dramatic shift from an agrarian to an industrial society. As technology developed in order to keep pace with the ever-increasing demands for consumer goods, the Industrial Revolution became a global phenomenon.

Kyoto Protocol: an attempt to reduce global warming by limiting carbon fuel emissions. Although the treaty was signed in 1997, enforcement did not begin until 2007. Several nations, notably the United States, refused to ratify the treaty.

Lilliputian: meaning "small," the word comes from a fictional race of miniature people mentioned in Jonathan Swift's *Gulliver's Travels*.

Linguistic turn: a development in Western philosophy that focused on the relationship between philosophy and language. This focus began in the early twentieth century as scholars suggested that part of what we thought of as reality was in fact a naming convention.

Little Ice Age: a period of cooling from around 1350 to 1750 that took place after the "late medieval warm period." It was caused in part by cyclical lows in solar radiation, volcanic activity, and changes in the circulation of ocean waters.

Manchurian War: a period of conflict in China during the seventeenth century. In 1644 the Manchus captured Beijing, overthrew the Ming dynasty, and began to consolidate their hold over the entire country, ultimately establishing the Qing dynasty that lasted until 1912.

Marxism: the social analysis of the nineteenth-century German political philosopher Karl Marx, according to which history is principally driven by class struggle. The political system of communism is largely derived from his theoretical work in economics and society.

Migration Period: a period of human migration of Germanic and Slavic tribes into Roman territory that occurred in Europe between around 300 and 700 c.e. It marks the start of the Early Middle Ages.

Mughal India: the territory of the Mughal Empire that extended from Persia into a large part of the Indian subcontinent and that existed between the sixteenth and eighteenth centuries.

Ottoman Empire: an empire that encompassed modern-day Turkey, western Asia, North Africa, and the Caucasus. Founded in 1299, it was finally dissolved in 1922.

Paleoclimatology: the study of changes in the climate over the entire history of the earth.

Palynology: the study of particles that can be collected in order to learn about the past. In particular, pollen can be used to build up a picture of vegetation in a particular area at any given time.

Past & Present: an American journal of history founded in 1952. Its original contributors tended toward Marxist philosophies.

Protestant: the second largest branch of the Christian faith, founded in the sixteenth century following the Reformation and its split from the Roman Catholic Church. Protestants reject the primacy of the pope and the significance of certain rituals, contrary to Roman Catholic doctrine.

Reformation: the split between the Roman Catholic and Protestant branches of the Christian religion in the sixteenth century instigated by Martin Luther and other Protestant reformers.

Roman Catholic: the largest branch of the Christian religion, headed by the pope, a figure believed by Catholics to be the direct successor to St Peter, martyred in the first century; Catholicism differs from Protestantism in certain rituals and points of doctrine.

Sociology: the study of social behavior and the history and functioning of human society.

Soviet Union (1917–91): a political union of communist states that was dominated by Russia. It was formed out of the ashes of the Russian Revolution of 1917 and dominated Eastern Europe until its collapse in 1991.

Speleothem: a natural deposit found in caves often in the form of stalagmites and stalactites. As with tree rings, banding can be found within these formations that reveals important information about events in the past.

Sunspots: dark spots on the surface of the sun caused by fluctuations in the sun's magnetic field. Visible from earth only by means of a telescope, an absence of or reduction in the number of sunspots usually indicates a reduction in the amount of solar energy that the earth receives.

Thirty Years War: a series of wars that took place between 1618 and 1648—effectively a European civil war that dragged in most of the major powers of the day, including England, France, Spain, and Sweden. Ostensibly a conflict between Protestantism and Catholicism, it eventually degenerated into a dynastic struggle between the French and Hapsburg rulers of Europe.

Tokugawa Japan: an era of Japanese history from 1602 to 1868, also known as the Edo period, that derives its name from its first political and military leader, Tokugawa Ieyasu.

Vandals: part of a Germanic tribe that sacked the city of Rome in 455 C.E. The kingdom collapsed in 533 C.E.

Western Roman Empire: an empire that existed from around 44 B.C.E. to 476 C.E. when the western half of the empire fell. The split between the eastern and western realms occurred in 395 C.E. when Emperor Theodosius I divided the empire between his two sons.

World War II (1939–45): a global conflict fought between the Axis Powers (Germany, Italy, and Japan) and the victorious Allied Powers (the United Kingdom and its colonies, the former Soviet Union, and the United States).

PEOPLE MENTIONED IN THE TEXT

Fernand Braudel (1902–85) was a French historian most closely associated with the *Annales* school of thought, which he helped to develop.

John L. Brooke (b. 1953) is an American historian. He graduated from Cornell in 1975 and is currently humanities distinguished professor of history at Ohio State University and director of OSU's Center for Historical Research.

Neville Brown (b. 1932) is a doctor of science in applied geophysics (geophysics is scientific inquiry into the earth's physics). A senior member of Mansfield College in Oxford, he is noted for his cross-disciplinary work in humanities and physics, particularly in certain aspects of meteorology.

Ulf Büntgen is a Swiss climatologist who currently works at the Swiss Institute for Forest, Snow and Landscape Research. He is an expert in dendrochronology, the tree-ring data that Parker made extensive use of.

Charles I (1600–49) was king of England, Scotland, and Ireland from 1625 until his execution by parliamentarians at the conclusion of the English Civil War.

Dagomar Degroot is an assistant professor of environmental history at Georgetown University. He received his PhD from York University in 2014.

Jan de Vries is the Ehrman Professor of the graduate school at the University of California, Berkeley. His fields of inquiry include seventeenth-century European social and economic history.

John A. Eddy (1931–2009) was an American astronomer best known for his discovery of the Maunder minimum, a 70-year period from 1645 to 1715 when solar activity was unusually low.

Ronnie Ellenblum is a professor at the Hebrew University of Jerusalem. His principle field of study is the history and archaeology of the Crusades, and in urban geographical history and environmental history.

John Huxtable Elliott (b. 1930) is an English historian and regius professor emeritus at Oxford University. He is principally known for his study of the Iberian Peninsula and was knighted for his contribution to history in 1994.

J. R. Fleming is a climatologist. Currently Charles A. Dana professor and director of science, technology, and society at Colby College in the US state of Maine, his many books and papers include *Inventing Atmospheric Science: Bjerknes, Rossby, Wexler, and the Foundations of Modern Meteorology* (2016) and *Fixing the Sky: The Checkered History of Weather and Climate Control* (2010).

Jack Goldstone (b. 1953) is an American sociologist who specializes in the field of revolutions and international politics. He is the current Virginia E. and John T. Hazel, Jr. Professor at George Mason University.

Thomas Hobbes (1588–1679) was an English philosopher of politics, mathematician and author of *Leviathan*, among other works. He is most famous for arguing that the state exists because in a state of nature everyone would constantly fear death. Consequently, society requires the establishment of an all-powerful Leviathan, or ruler, to set the laws and customs that will prevent civil war.

Eric Hobsbawm (1917–2012) was a British Marxist historian. His principle areas of study were the rise of capitalism, socialism, and nationalism.

James II (1633–1701) was king of England, Scotland, and Ireland from 1685 to 1688. Suspected of being pro-French and pro-Catholic, he was deposed in favor of a limited, and explicitly Protestant, monarchy in the Glorious Revolution of 1688.

Morgan Kelly is a professor of economics at the University of Dublin. His research interests include property-price markets and economic history.

Genghis Khan (1162–1227) was the founder of the Mongol Empire, one of the largest empires of all time that, at its height, stretched from central Europe to the Sea of Japan.

Emmanuel Le Roy Ladurie (b. 1929) is a French historian whose principle focus is the Ancien Regime and the history of the peasantry. He is Emeritus Professor at the Collège de France.

Stephan Lewandowsky (b. 1958) is an Australian psychologist. He currently works at Bristol University, where he holds the chair in cognitive psychology.

Mary Lindemann (b. 1949) is an American historian who specializes in early modern German, Dutch, and Flemish history. She is the current professor of history at the Miami College of Arts and Science.

Karl Marx (1818–83) was a German economist and philosopher, and the preeminent theorist of communism; his major work is *Das Kapital* (1867–94). The young Marx was a "young Hegelian" thinker.

J. R. McNeill (b. 1954) is an American historian and professor at Georgetown University. His principle research is in the area of environmental history.

Henry Oldenburg (1619–77) was a German religious scholar noted as the founder of the modern practice of scientific peer review—the process by which scientific papers are evaluated by scientists working in an appropriate field.

Count-Duke of Olivares (1587–1645) also known as Gasper De Guzman was the chief minister in the court of Philip IV of Spain from 1621 to 1643.

Naomi Oreskes (b. 1958) is an American historian of science and economic geology. She is coauthor, with Erik M. Conway, of the 2010 book *Merchants of Doubt*.

Anthony Pagden (b. 1945) is a professor of history and political science in UCLA's department of political science.

Christian Pfister (1857–1933) was a French historian who focused on the history of urbanization with particular reference to the French town of Nancy and the historical importance of the Alsace Lorraine region of France.

Phillip II (1527–98) was the king of Spain and later Portugal, one of the most powerful men alive in the seventeenth century. He was also briefly king of England and Ireland due to his marriage to Mary I in 1554. He is perhaps best remembered for the failed invasion of England known as the Spanish Armada in 1588.

Kenneth Pomeranz (b. 1958) is a professor of modern Chinese history at the University of Chicago. He received his PhD from Yale University in 1988.

Theodore K. Rabb (b. 1937) is an American historian whose main focus of study is the early modern period. He currently holds the post of emeritus professor of history at Princeton University.

Niels Steensgaard (1932–2013) was a Danish historian whose main focus of interest lay in the early modern period of around 1400–1700. He taught at the University of Copenhagen in Denmark from 1977 to 2002.

Joseph A. Tainter (b. 1949) is an American historian and anthropologist. His best-known work is *The Collapse of Complex Societies* (1990).

Julia Adeney Thomas is an associate professor of history at the University of Notre Dame. Her principle areas of study are the political history of Japan and environmental history's impact on historiography.

Tokugawa Iemitsu (1604–51) was the third person to take on the title of *Shogun* (military leader) of Japan and ruled from 1623 until 1651.

Hugh Trevor-Roper (1914–2003) was a British historian best known for his work on early modern history and Nazi Germany. He held the post of regius professor of modern history at Oxford University between 1957 and 1980, and in 1979 was introduced to the House of Lords as Baron Dacre of Glanton.

Markus Vink is a professor of history at the State University of New York at Fredonia. His principle areas of study are the slave trade, military history, and "modern" trade systems.

Voltaire was the pen-name of **François-Marie Arouet (1694– 1778),** a French philosopher of the Enlightenment. During his career he attacked the Catholic Church, and championed freedom of speech and religion.

Aono Yasayuki is a research professor at the University of Osaka Prefecture University. Her research interests include geography and agricultural environmental engineering.

WORKS CITED

WORKS CITED

Benedikter Roland, Eugene Codero, and Anne Marie Todd. "The 'American Way of Life' and US Views on Climate Change and the Environment." In *Cultural Dynamics of Climate Change and the Environment in Northern America*, edited by Bernd Sommer. Leiden, Netherlands: Brill Publishing, 2015.

Brooke, John. L. *Climate Change and the Course of Global History: A Rough Journey.* New York: Cambridge University Press, 2014.

Brown, Neville. *History and Climate Change: A Eurocentric Perspective*. New York: Routledge, 2014.

Büntgen, Ulf, Willy Tegel, Kurt Nicolussi, Michael McCormick, David Frank, Valerie Trouet, Jed O. Kaplan, Franz Herzig, Karl-Uwe Heussner, Heinz Wanner, Jürg Luterbacher, and Jab Esper. "2500 Years of European Climate Variability and Human Susceptibility." *Science* 331, no. 6017 (2011): 578–82.

Degroot, Dagomar. "Review: *Global Crisis: War, Climate Change and Catastrophe in the Seventeenth Century.*" *E-International Relations* (2014). Accessed October 6, 2015. http://www.e-ir.info/2014/12/12/review-global-crisis-war-climate-change-catastrophe-in-the-17th-century.

De Vries, Jan "The Crisis of the Seventeenth Century: The Little Ice Age and the Mystery of the Great Divergence." *Journal of Interdisciplinary History* 44, no. 3 (2014): 369–77.

Eddy, John A. "The Maunder Minimum: Sunspots and Climate in the Reign of Louis XIV." In *The General Crisis of the Seventeenth Century,* edited by Geoffrey Parker and Lesley M. Smith. 2nd edn. London: Routledge, 1997.

Ellenblum, Ronnie. *The Collapse of the Eastern Mediterranean: Climate Change and the Decline of the East, 950–1072.* Cambridge: Cambridge University Press, 2012.

Elliott, J. H. "The General Crisis in Retrospect: A Debate without End." In *Early Modern Europe: From Crises to Stability,* edited by Philip Benedict and Myron P. Gutmann. Newark, DE: University of Delaware Press, 2005.

Fagan, Brian M. *The Little Ice Age: How Climate Made History 1300–1850.* New York: Basic Books, 2000.

Fleming, James Rodger. *Historical Perspectives on Climate Change.* New York and Oxford: Oxford University Press, 1998.

Fredrichs, R. Christopher. "The War in Myth, Legend and History." In *The Thirty Years War,* edited by Geoffrey Parker. 2nd edn. New York: Routledge, 1997.

Goldstone, Jack A. "Climate Lessons from History." *Historically Speaking* 14, no. 5 (2013): 35–7.

Google Scholar. "Parker Global Crisis." Accessed September 29, 2015. https://scholar.google.com/scholar?hl=en&q=Parker+Global+Crisis&btnG=&as_sdt=1%2C9&as_sdtp=.

Hill, Christopher, R. H. Hilton, and E. J. Hobsbawm. "*Past & Present*: Origins and Early Years." *Past & Present* 100, no. 1 (1983): 3–14.

Historynet. "Interview with Author-Historian Geoffrey Parker" (2013). Accessed October 21, 2015. http://www.historynet.com/interview-with-author-historian-geoffrey-parker.htm.

Hobbes, Thomas. *Leviathan,* edited by Richard Tuck. Cambridge: Cambridge University Press, 1996.

Hobsbawm, E. J. "The General Crisis of the European Economy in the Seventeenth Century." *Past & Present* 5, no. 1 (1954): 33–53.

Huntington, Ellsworth. "Climate Change and Agricultural Exhaustion as Elements in the Fall of Rome." *Quarterly Journal of Economics* 33, no. 2 (1917): 173–208.

Intergovernmental Panel on Climate Change. *Fourth Assessment Impact Report*, 2007. Accessed October 16, 2015. http://www.ipcc.ch/publications_and_data/ar4/syr/en/spms3.html.

Kelly, Morgan, and Cormac Ó Gráda. "The Waning of the Little Ice Age: Climate Change in Early Modern Europe." *Journal of Interdisciplinary History* 44, no. 3 (2014): 301–25.

Le Goff, Jacques. "Later History," *Past & Present* 100, no. 1 (1983): 14–28.

Lewandowsky, Stephan, Naomi Oreskes, James S. Risbey, Ben R. Newell, and Michael Smithson. "Seepage: Climate Change Denial and Its Effect on the Scientific Community." *Global Environmental Change* 33, (2015): 1–13.

Lindemann, Mary. "*Global Crisis: War, Climate Change and Catastrophe in the Seventeenth Century* by Geoffrey Parker." *German Studies Review* 38, no. 1 (2015): 157–9.

McNeill, J. R. "Maunder Minimum and Parker Maximum." *Historically Speaking* 14, no. 5 (2013): 34–5.

Ohio State University, Department of History. "Geoffrey Parker." Accessed September 3, 2015. http://history.osu.edu/directory/Parker277.

Oreskes Naomi. "Beyond the Ivory Tower: The Scientific Consensus on Climate Change." *Science* 306, no. 5702 (2004): 1686.

Pagden, Anthony. "*Global Crisis: War, Climate Change and Catastrophe in the Seventeenth Century* by Geoffrey Parker (review)." *Common Knowledge* 21, no. 3 (2015): 515–16.

Parker, Geoffrey. *The Army of Flanders and the Spanish Road 1567–1659.* 2nd edn. Cambridge: Cambridge University Press, 2004.

——— "Crisis and Catastrophe: The Global Crisis of the Seventeenth Century Reconsidered." *American Historical Review* 113, no. 4 (2008): 1053–79.

——— *The Dutch Revolt.* Ithaca, NY: Cornell University Press 1977.

——— *Europe in Crisis, 1598–1648.* 2nd edn. Oxford: Blackwell Publishers Ltd. 1990.

——— *Global Crisis: War, Climate Change and Catastrophe in the Seventeenth Century.* New Haven and London: Yale University Press, 2013.

——— *The Military Revolution: Military Innovation and the Rise of the West 1500–1800.* 2nd edn. Cambridge: Cambridge University Press, 1996.

——— "Response." *Historically Speaking* 14, no. 5 (2013): 38–9.

——— *The World is Not Enough: The Imperial Vision of Philip II of Spain* (Waco, TX: Baylor University Press, 2000).

Parker, Geoffrey, ed. *The Thirty Years War.* 2nd edn. New York: Routledge, 1997.

Parker, Geoffrey, and Lesley M. Smith, eds. *The General Crisis of the Seventeenth Century.* 2nd edn. London: Routledge 1997.

Pfister, Christian. "Weather, Climate, and the Environment." In *The Oxford Handbook of Early Modern European History, 1350–1750,* edited by Hamish Scott. Oxford: Oxford University Press, 2015.

Pfister, Christian, Rudolf Brazdil, and Rudiger Glaser, eds. *Climatic Variability in Sixteenth-Century Europe and Its Social Dimension.* Dordrecht: Springer Science, 1999.

Pomeranz, Kenneth. "Weather, War, and Welfare: Persistence and Change in Geoffrey Parker's *Global Crisis.*" *Historically Speaking* 14, no. 5 (2013): 30–3.

Post, John D. *The Last Great Subsistence Crisis in the Western World.* Baltimore: Johns Hopkins University Press, 1977.

Rabb, Theodore, K. *The Struggle for Stability in Early Modern Europe.* New York: Oxford University Press, 1975.

Reith, Reinhold. *Umweltgeschichte der frühen Neuzeit* (An Environmental History of the Early Modern Period). Munich: Oldenbourg, 2011.

Scott, Hamish. "Introduction: Early Modern Europe and the Idea of 'Early

Modernity.'" In *The Oxford Handbook of Early Modern European History, 1350–1750*, edited by Hamish Scott. Oxford: Oxford University Press, 2015.

Steensgaard, Niels. "The Seventeenth-Century Crisis." In *The General Crisis of the Seventeenth Century*, edited by Geoffrey Parker and Lesley M. Smith. 2nd edn. London: Routledge, 1997.

Tainter, Joseph A. "Global Change, History and Sustainability." In *The Way the Wind Blows: Climate History, and Human Action*, edited by Roderick J. McIntosh, Joseph A. Tainter, and Susan Keech Mcintosh. New York: Columbia University Press, 2000.

Thomas, Julia Adeney. "Not Yet Far Enough." *American Historical Review* 117, no. 3 (2012): 794–803.

Trevor-Roper, Hugh. "The General Crisis of the Seventeenth Century." *Past & Present* 16, no. 1 (1959): 31–64.

Vink, Markus "Review: *Global Crisis: War, Climate Change and Catastrophe in the Seventeenth Century* by Geoffrey Parker." *Journal of Modern History* 86, no. 3 (2014): 640–2.

Yasayuki, Aono. "Cherry Blossom Phenological Data since the Seventeenth Century for Edo (Tokyo), Japan, and Their Application to Estimation of March Temperatures." *International Journal of Biometeorology* 59, no. 4 (2015): 427–34.

THE MACAT LIBRARY
BY DISCIPLINE

AFRICANA STUDIES

Chinua Achebe's *An Image of Africa: Racism in Conrad's Heart of Darkness*
W. E. B. Du Bois's *The Souls of Black Folk*
Zora Neale Huston's *Characteristics of Negro Expression*
Martin Luther King Jr's *Why We Can't Wait*
Toni Morrison's *Playing in the Dark: Whiteness in the American Literary Imagination*

ANTHROPOLOGY

Arjun Appadurai's *Modernity at Large: Cultural Dimensions of Globalisation*
Philippe Ariès's *Centuries of Childhood*
Franz Boas's *Race, Language and Culture*
Kim Chan & Renée Mauborgne's *Blue Ocean Strategy*
Jared Diamond's *Guns, Germs & Steel: the Fate of Human Societies*
Jared Diamond's *Collapse: How Societies Choose to Fail or Survive*
E. E. Evans-Pritchard's *Witchcraft, Oracles and Magic Among the Azande*
James Ferguson's *The Anti-Politics Machine*
Clifford Geertz's *The Interpretation of Cultures*
David Graeber's *Debt: the First 5000 Years*
Karen Ho's *Liquidated: An Ethnography of Wall Street*
Geert Hofstede's *Culture's Consequences: Comparing Values, Behaviors, Institutes and Organizations across Nations*
Claude Lévi-Strauss's *Structural Anthropology*
Jay Macleod's *Ain't No Makin' It: Aspirations and Attainment in a Low-Income Neighborhood*
Saba Mahmood's *The Politics of Piety: The Islamic Revival and the Feminist Subject*
Marcel Mauss's *The Gift*

BUSINESS

Jean Lave & Etienne Wenger's *Situated Learning*
Theodore Levitt's *Marketing Myopia*
Burton G. Malkiel's *A Random Walk Down Wall Street*
Douglas McGregor's *The Human Side of Enterprise*
Michael Porter's *Competitive Strategy: Creating and Sustaining Superior Performance*
John Kotter's *Leading Change*
C. K. Prahalad & Gary Hamel's *The Core Competence of the Corporation*

CRIMINOLOGY

Michelle Alexander's *The New Jim Crow: Mass Incarceration in the Age of Colorblindness*
Michael R. Gottfredson & Travis Hirschi's *A General Theory of Crime*
Richard Herrnstein & Charles A. Murray's *The Bell Curve: Intelligence and Class Structure in American Life*
Elizabeth Loftus's *Eyewitness Testimony*
Jay Macleod's *Ain't No Makin' It: Aspirations and Attainment in a Low-Income Neighborhood*
Philip Zimbardo's *The Lucifer Effect*

ECONOMICS

Janet Abu-Lughod's *Before European Hegemony*
Ha-Joon Chang's *Kicking Away the Ladder*
David Brion Davis's *The Problem of Slavery in the Age of Revolution*
Milton Friedman's *The Role of Monetary Policy*
Milton Friedman's *Capitalism and Freedom*
David Graeber's *Debt: the First 5000 Years*
Friedrich Hayek's *The Road to Serfdom*
Karen Ho's *Liquidated: An Ethnography of Wall Street*

John Maynard Keynes's *The General Theory of Employment, Interest and Money*
Charles P. Kindleberger's *Manias, Panics and Crashes*
Robert Lucas's *Why Doesn't Capital Flow from Rich to Poor Countries?*
Burton G. Malkiel's *A Random Walk Down Wall Street*
Thomas Robert Malthus's *An Essay on the Principle of Population*
Karl Marx's *Capital*
Thomas Piketty's *Capital in the Twenty-First Century*
Amartya Sen's *Development as Freedom*
Adam Smith's *The Wealth of Nations*
Nassim Nicholas Taleb's *The Black Swan: The Impact of the Highly Improbable*
Amos Tversky's & Daniel Kahneman's *Judgment under Uncertainty: Heuristics and Biases*
Mahbub Ul Haq's *Reflections on Human Development*
Max Weber's *The Protestant Ethic and the Spirit of Capitalism*

FEMINISM AND GENDER STUDIES

Judith Butler's *Gender Trouble*
Simone De Beauvoir's *The Second Sex*
Michel Foucault's *History of Sexuality*
Betty Friedan's *The Feminine Mystique*
Saba Mahmood's *The Politics of Piety: The Islamic Revival and the Feminist Subject*
Joan Wallach Scott's *Gender and the Politics of History*
Mary Wollstonecraft's *A Vindication of the Rights of Women*
Virginia Woolf's *A Room of One's Own*

GEOGRAPHY

The Brundtland Report's *Our Common Future*
Rachel Carson's *Silent Spring*
Charles Darwin's *On the Origin of Species*
James Ferguson's *The Anti-Politics Machine*
Jane Jacobs's *The Death and Life of Great American Cities*
James Lovelock's *Gaia: A New Look at Life on Earth*
Amartya Sen's *Development as Freedom*
Mathis Wackernagel & William Rees's *Our Ecological Footprint*

HISTORY

Janet Abu-Lughod's *Before European Hegemony*
Benedict Anderson's *Imagined Communities*
Bernard Bailyn's *The Ideological Origins of the American Revolution*
Hanna Batatu's *The Old Social Classes And The Revolutionary Movements Of Iraq*
Christopher Browning's *Ordinary Men: Reserve Police Batallion 101 and the Final Solution in Poland*
Edmund Burke's *Reflections on the Revolution in France*
William Cronon's *Nature's Metropolis: Chicago And The Great West*
Alfred W. Crosby's *The Columbian Exchange*
Hamid Dabashi's *Iran: A People Interrupted*
David Brion Davis's *The Problem of Slavery in the Age of Revolution*
Nathalie Zemon Davis's *The Return of Martin Guerre*
Jared Diamond's *Guns, Germs & Steel: the Fate of Human Societies*
Frank Dikotter's *Mao's Great Famine*
John W Dower's *War Without Mercy: Race And Power In The Pacific War*
W. E. B. Du Bois's *The Souls of Black Folk*
Richard J. Evans's *In Defence of History*
Lucien Febvre's *The Problem of Unbelief in the 16th Century*
Sheila Fitzpatrick's *Everyday Stalinism*

The Macat Library By Discipline

Eric Foner's *Reconstruction: America's Unfinished Revolution, 1863-1877*
Michel Foucault's *Discipline and Punish*
Michel Foucault's *History of Sexuality*
Francis Fukuyama's *The End of History and the Last Man*
John Lewis Gaddis's *We Now Know: Rethinking Cold War History*
Ernest Gellner's *Nations and Nationalism*
Eugene Genovese's *Roll, Jordan, Roll: The World the Slaves Made*
Carlo Ginzburg's *The Night Battles*
Daniel Goldhagen's *Hitler's Willing Executioners*
Jack Goldstone's *Revolution and Rebellion in the Early Modern World*
Antonio Gramsci's *The Prison Notebooks*
Alexander Hamilton, John Jay & James Madison's *The Federalist Papers*
Christopher Hill's *The World Turned Upside Down*
Carole Hillenbrand's *The Crusades: Islamic Perspectives*
Thomas Hobbes's *Leviathan*
Eric Hobsbawm's *The Age Of Revolution*
John A. Hobson's *Imperialism: A Study*
Albert Hourani's *History of the Arab Peoples*
Samuel P. Huntington's *The Clash of Civilizations and the Remaking of World Order*
C. L. R. James's *The Black Jacobins*
Tony Judt's *Postwar: A History of Europe Since 1945*
Ernst Kantorowicz's *The King's Two Bodies: A Study in Medieval Political Theology*
Paul Kennedy's *The Rise and Fall of the Great Powers*
Ian Kershaw's *The "Hitler Myth": Image and Reality in the Third Reich*
John Maynard Keynes's *The General Theory of Employment, Interest and Money*
Charles P. Kindleberger's *Manias, Panics and Crashes*
Martin Luther King Jr's *Why We Can't Wait*
Henry Kissinger's *World Order: Reflections on the Character of Nations and the Course of History*
Thomas Kuhn's *The Structure of Scientific Revolutions*
Georges Lefebvre's *The Coming of the French Revolution*
John Locke's *Two Treatises of Government*
Niccolò Machiavelli's *The Prince*
Thomas Robert Malthus's *An Essay on the Principle of Population*
Mahmood Mamdani's *Citizen and Subject: Contemporary Africa And The Legacy Of Late Colonialism*
Karl Marx's *Capital*
Stanley Milgram's *Obedience to Authority*
John Stuart Mill's *On Liberty*
Thomas Paine's *Common Sense*
Thomas Paine's *Rights of Man*
Geoffrey Parker's *Global Crisis: War, Climate Change and Catastrophe in the Seventeenth Century*
Jonathan Riley-Smith's *The First Crusade and the Idea of Crusading*
Jean-Jacques Rousseau's *The Social Contract*
Joan Wallach Scott's *Gender and the Politics of History*
Theda Skocpol's *States and Social Revolutions*
Adam Smith's *The Wealth of Nations*
Timothy Snyder's *Bloodlands: Europe Between Hitler and Stalin*
Sun Tzu's *The Art of War*
Keith Thomas's *Religion and the Decline of Magic*
Thucydides's *The History of the Peloponnesian War*
Frederick Jackson Turner's *The Significance of the Frontier in American History*
Odd Arne Westad's *The Global Cold War: Third World Interventions And The Making Of Our Times*

LITERATURE

Chinua Achebe's *An Image of Africa: Racism in Conrad's Heart of Darkness*
Roland Barthes's *Mythologies*
Homi K. Bhabha's *The Location of Culture*
Judith Butler's *Gender Trouble*
Simone De Beauvoir's *The Second Sex*
Ferdinand De Saussure's *Course in General Linguistics*
T. S. Eliot's *The Sacred Wood: Essays on Poetry and Criticism*
Zora Neale Huston's *Characteristics of Negro Expression*
Toni Morrison's *Playing in the Dark: Whiteness in the American Literary Imagination*
Edward Said's *Orientalism*
Gayatri Chakravorty Spivak's *Can the Subaltern Speak?*
Mary Wollstonecraft's *A Vindication of the Rights of Women*
Virginia Woolf's *A Room of One's Own*

PHILOSOPHY

Elizabeth Anscombe's *Modern Moral Philosophy*
Hannah Arendt's *The Human Condition*
Aristotle's *Metaphysics*
Aristotle's *Nicomachean Ethics*
Edmund Gettier's *Is Justified True Belief Knowledge?*
Georg Wilhelm Friedrich Hegel's *Phenomenology of Spirit*
David Hume's *Dialogues Concerning Natural Religion*
David Hume's *The Enquiry for Human Understanding*
Immanuel Kant's *Religion within the Boundaries of Mere Reason*
Immanuel Kant's *Critique of Pure Reason*
Søren Kierkegaard's *The Sickness Unto Death*
Søren Kierkegaard's *Fear and Trembling*
C. S. Lewis's *The Abolition of Man*
Alasdair MacIntyre's *After Virtue*
Marcus Aurelius's *Meditations*
Friedrich Nietzsche's *On the Genealogy of Morality*
Friedrich Nietzsche's *Beyond Good and Evil*
Plato's *Republic*
Plato's *Symposium*
Jean-Jacques Rousseau's *The Social Contract*
Gilbert Ryle's *The Concept of Mind*
Baruch Spinoza's *Ethics*
Sun Tzu's *The Art of War*
Ludwig Wittgenstein's *Philosophical Investigations*

POLITICS

Benedict Anderson's *Imagined Communities*
Aristotle's *Politics*
Bernard Bailyn's *The Ideological Origins of the American Revolution*
Edmund Burke's *Reflections on the Revolution in France*
John C. Calhoun's *A Disquisition on Government*
Ha-Joon Chang's *Kicking Away the Ladder*
Hamid Dabashi's *Iran: A People Interrupted*
Hamid Dabashi's *Theology of Discontent: The Ideological Foundation of the Islamic Revolution in Iran*
Robert Dahl's *Democracy and its Critics*
Robert Dahl's *Who Governs?*
David Brion Davis's *The Problem of Slavery in the Age of Revolution*

Alexis De Tocqueville's *Democracy in America*
James Ferguson's *The Anti-Politics Machine*
Frank Dikotter's *Mao's Great Famine*
Sheila Fitzpatrick's *Everyday Stalinism*
Eric Foner's *Reconstruction: America's Unfinished Revolution, 1863-1877*
Milton Friedman's *Capitalism and Freedom*
Francis Fukuyama's *The End of History and the Last Man*
John Lewis Gaddis's *We Now Know: Rethinking Cold War History*
Ernest Gellner's *Nations and Nationalism*
David Graeber's *Debt: the First 5000 Years*
Antonio Gramsci's *The Prison Notebooks*
Alexander Hamilton, John Jay & James Madison's *The Federalist Papers*
Friedrich Hayek's *The Road to Serfdom*
Christopher Hill's *The World Turned Upside Down*
Thomas Hobbes's *Leviathan*
John A. Hobson's *Imperialism: A Study*
Samuel P. Huntington's *The Clash of Civilizations and the Remaking of World Order*
Tony Judt's *Postwar: A History of Europe Since 1945*
David C. Kang's *China Rising: Peace, Power and Order in East Asia*
Paul Kennedy's *The Rise and Fall of Great Powers*
Robert Keohane's *After Hegemony*
Martin Luther King Jr.'s *Why We Can't Wait*
Henry Kissinger's *World Order: Reflections on the Character of Nations and the Course of History*
John Locke's *Two Treatises of Government*
Niccolò Machiavelli's *The Prince*
Thomas Robert Malthus's *An Essay on the Principle of Population*
Mahmood Mamdani's *Citizen and Subject: Contemporary Africa And The Legacy Of Late Colonialism*
Karl Marx's *Capital*
John Stuart Mill's *On Liberty*
John Stuart Mill's *Utilitarianism*
Hans Morgenthau's *Politics Among Nations*
Thomas Paine's *Common Sense*
Thomas Paine's *Rights of Man*
Thomas Piketty's *Capital in the Twenty-First Century*
Robert D. Putman's *Bowling Alone*
John Rawls's *Theory of Justice*
Jean-Jacques Rousseau's *The Social Contract*
Theda Skocpol's *States and Social Revolutions*
Adam Smith's *The Wealth of Nations*
Sun Tzu's *The Art of War*
Henry David Thoreau's *Civil Disobedience*
Thucydides's *The History of the Peloponnesian War*
Kenneth Waltz's *Theory of International Politics*
Max Weber's *Politics as a Vocation*
Odd Arne Westad's *The Global Cold War: Third World Interventions And The Making Of Our Times*

POSTCOLONIAL STUDIES

Roland Barthes's *Mythologies*
Frantz Fanon's *Black Skin, White Masks*
Homi K. Bhabha's *The Location of Culture*
Gustavo Gutiérrez's *A Theology of Liberation*
Edward Said's *Orientalism*
Gayatri Chakravorty Spivak's *Can the Subaltern Speak?*

PSYCHOLOGY

Gordon Allport's *The Nature of Prejudice*
Alan Baddeley & Graham Hitch's *Aggression: A Social Learning Analysis*
Albert Bandura's *Aggression: A Social Learning Analysis*
Leon Festinger's *A Theory of Cognitive Dissonance*
Sigmund Freud's *The Interpretation of Dreams*
Betty Friedan's *The Feminine Mystique*
Michael R. Gottfredson & Travis Hirschi's *A General Theory of Crime*
Eric Hoffer's *The True Believer: Thoughts on the Nature of Mass Movements*
William James's *Principles of Psychology*
Elizabeth Loftus's *Eyewitness Testimony*
A. H. Maslow's *A Theory of Human Motivation*
Stanley Milgram's *Obedience to Authority*
Steven Pinker's *The Better Angels of Our Nature*
Oliver Sacks's *The Man Who Mistook His Wife For a Hat*
Richard Thaler & Cass Sunstein's *Nudge: Improving Decisions About Health, Wealth and Happiness*
Amos Tversky's *Judgment under Uncertainty: Heuristics and Biases*
Philip Zimbardo's *The Lucifer Effect*

SCIENCE

Rachel Carson's *Silent Spring*
William Cronon's *Nature's Metropolis: Chicago And The Great West*
Alfred W. Crosby's *The Columbian Exchange*
Charles Darwin's *On the Origin of Species*
Richard Dawkin's *The Selfish Gene*
Thomas Kuhn's *The Structure of Scientific Revolutions*
Geoffrey Parker's *Global Crisis: War, Climate Change and Catastrophe in the Seventeenth Century*
Mathis Wackernagel & William Rees's *Our Ecological Footprint*

SOCIOLOGY

Michelle Alexander's *The New Jim Crow: Mass Incarceration in the Age of Colorblindness*
Gordon Allport's *The Nature of Prejudice*
Albert Bandura's *Aggression: A Social Learning Analysis*
Hanna Batatu's *The Old Social Classes And The Revolutionary Movements Of Iraq*
Ha-Joon Chang's *Kicking Away the Ladder*
W. E. B. Du Bois's *The Souls of Black Folk*
Émile Durkheim's *On Suicide*
Frantz Fanon's *Black Skin, White Masks*
Frantz Fanon's *The Wretched of the Earth*
Eric Foner's *Reconstruction: America's Unfinished Revolution, 1863-1877*
Eugene Genovese's *Roll, Jordan, Roll: The World the Slaves Made*
Jack Goldstone's *Revolution and Rebellion in the Early Modern World*
Antonio Gramsci's *The Prison Notebooks*
Richard Herrnstein & Charles A Murray's *The Bell Curve: Intelligence and Class Structure in American Life*
Eric Hoffer's *The True Believer: Thoughts on the Nature of Mass Movements*
Jane Jacobs's *The Death and Life of Great American Cities*
Robert Lucas's *Why Doesn't Capital Flow from Rich to Poor Countries?*
Jay Macleod's *Ain't No Makin' It: Aspirations and Attainment in a Low Income Neighborhood*
Elaine May's *Homeward Bound: American Families in the Cold War Era*
Douglas McGregor's *The Human Side of Enterprise*
C. Wright Mills's *The Sociological Imagination*

The Macat Library By Discipline

Thomas Piketty's *Capital in the Twenty-First Century*
Robert D. Putman's *Bowling Alone*
David Riesman's *The Lonely Crowd: A Study of the Changing American Character*
Edward Said's *Orientalism*
Joan Wallach Scott's *Gender and the Politics of History*
Theda Skocpol's *States and Social Revolutions*
Max Weber's *The Protestant Ethic and the Spirit of Capitalism*

THEOLOGY

Augustine's *Confessions*
Benedict's *Rule of St Benedict*
Gustavo Gutiérrez's *A Theology of Liberation*
Carole Hillenbrand's *The Crusades: Islamic Perspectives*
David Hume's *Dialogues Concerning Natural Religion*
Immanuel Kant's *Religion within the Boundaries of Mere Reason*
Ernst Kantorowicz's *The King's Two Bodies: A Study in Medieval Political Theology*
Søren Kierkegaard's *The Sickness Unto Death*
C. S. Lewis's *The Abolition of Man*
Saba Mahmood's *The Politics of Piety: The Islamic Revival and the Feminist Subject*
Baruch Spinoza's *Ethics*
Keith Thomas's *Religion and the Decline of Magic*

COMING SOON

Chris Argyris's *The Individual and the Organisation*
Seyla Benhabib's *The Rights of Others*
Walter Benjamin's *The Work Of Art in the Age of Mechanical Reproduction*
John Berger's *Ways of Seeing*
Pierre Bourdieu's *Outline of a Theory of Practice*
Mary Douglas's *Purity and Danger*
Roland Dworkin's *Taking Rights Seriously*
James G. March's *Exploration and Exploitation in Organisational Learning*
Ikujiro Nonaka's *A Dynamic Theory of Organizational Knowledge Creation*
Griselda Pollock's *Vision and Difference*
Amartya Sen's *Inequality Re-Examined*
Susan Sontag's *On Photography*
Yasser Tabbaa's *The Transformation of Islamic Art*
Ludwig von Mises's *Theory of Money and Credit*

.